THE NEW
BOSTON
BUCKET LIST

100 WAYS TO HAVE A REAL BOSTON, MASSACHUSETTS EXPERIENCE

Larry Stanford

LEGAL DISCLAIMER

This book is designed to provide information, entertainment, and motivation to our readers. It is sold with the understanding that the publisher is not engaged to render any type of physical, psychological, legal, or any other kind of professional advice.

Participation in the activities listed may be dangerous or illegal and could lead to arrest, serious injury, or death.

The content of this book is the sole expression and opinion of its author and not necessarily that of the publisher. No warranties or guarantees are expressed or implied.

Neither the publisher nor the individual author shall be liable for any physical, psychological, emotional, financial, or commercial damages, including, but not limited to, special, incidental, consequential, or other damages. Our views and rights are the same: you are responsible for your own choices, actions, and results.

Why a bucket list?
What to expect
1. No Instruction Manual:

I've never been a fan of the instructional guidebook that tells you what to do and how to do it with tips for the best results. I know what I like. Tell me something worth doing, and I'll tailor it to my desires. That's the approach I'm taking here. Once you get a few check marks under your belt, you will understand why.

2. Adventure & Challenge:

Consider the list a primer for adventure. Some tasks are easy to accomplish, some are difficult, and some are close to impossible. The mix is intended to introduce you to new experiences in unique locations that define Boston. Take things at your own pace. No one is grading your performance.

3. Satisfaction:

Whether you fill the list at the end with fat red check marks and seek out every adventure from 1-100 or just take the journeys in your mind from the comfort of your favorite chair, this book should leave you with a sense of satisfaction. Life is about evolving and a little constructive criticism can go a long way. Feeling supercharged? Want to share your adventures with others? There's a place for that, too.

Enjoy, Larry

A special thanks to the Commissioner of Audio Visual, Craft Beers, Fine Cheeses and Small Market Baseball Teams for his ideas and suggestions for the Boston Bucket List.

Table of Contents

1

ONE IF BY LAND, TWO IF BY SEA

WHAT'S THE DEAL? The oldest standing church in Boston, is The Old North Church. This is the location of the famous saying where Paul Revere ordered lit lanterns to be displayed from the spire to warn the Patriots on the Charlestown side of the river about British troop movements.

DO IT IF: You are amazed by revolutionary war sites and American History.

SKIP IT IF: You believe the colonies should have remained loyal to the crown.

LOCAL ADVICE: The Old North Church is both a national historic landmark operated by the Old North Foundation and an active Episcopal Church congregation. Established in 1723 as Christ Church in the City of Boston, Old North is the oldest church building and the longest serving Episcopal congregation in the City. One neat aspect of the church are the numbered pews which were owned by famous and infamous churchgoers.

I DID IT: ☐ Oldnorth.com

DID YOU KNOW?

The enduring fame of the Old North began on the evening of April 18, 1775, when the church sexton, Robert Newman, and Vestryman Capt. John Pulling, Jr. climbed the steeple and held high two lanterns as a signal from Paul Revere that the British were marching to Lexington and Concord by sea across the Charles River and not by land. This fateful event ignited the American Revolution.

2

TRAVERSE THE FREEDOM TRAIL

WHAT'S THE DEAL? This 2.5 walk passes 16 of Boston's most significant historic sites, starting at the Boston Common and winding north to the U.S.S. Constitution. Most of the trail is marked by red painted bricks for an easy-to-follow route.

DO IT IF: You crave walks through 17th and 18th century landmarks and neighborhoods.

SKIP IT if: 2.5 miles is a long walk for you.

LOCAL ADVICE: Taking a guided walk with a costumed guide is a great way to learn not only about the historical landmarks, but about the people who shaped our new nation. Tours meet at the Boston Common visitor's center and travel about 1.5 of the 2.5-mile trail.

I DID IT: ☐ Thefreedomtrail.org

DID YOU KNOW?

The Freedom Trail was conceived by local journalist William Schofield, who in 1951 suggested building a pedestrian trail to link important local landmarks. Boston mayor John Hynes decided to put Schofield's idea into action. By 1953, 40,000 people were walking the trail annually.

3

WATCH A SOX GAME FROM THE MONSTER SEATS

WHAT'S THE DEAL? In 2003, seats were added atop Fenway Parks' famous outfield wall, the Green Monster. Only 310 feet from home plate, the 37-foot-high wall offers unique views of the Red Sox home field since 1912.

DO IT IF: You want to view a historic ballpark from a unique angle.

SKIP IT IF: You are visiting Boston on a budget; these seats are quite expensive.

LOCAL ADVICE: Plan your visit to Fenway Park far ahead because these seats are in big demand from locals and tourists alike. Keep in mind the Red Sox opponents play a huge part in the ticket prices as well. When the rival Yankees are in town, ticket demand skyrockets!

I DID IT: ☐ www.mlb.com/redsox/ballpark

DID YOU KNOW?

The 37-foot-high wall was part of the original construction in 1914, was made of wood and was a giant advertising billboard until 1947. That is when it was finally painted green. High walls at Baseball parks were common to keep out peeping eyes and force locals to purchase tickets to see the games.

4

KAYAK THE CHARLES

WHAT'S THE DEAL? There is a 9 mile stretch of the Charles River, which divides Boston and Cambridge that has almost no current. This allows easy paddling and offers views of the downtown Boston skyline, the Zakim Bridge and MIT's campus. Kayak rentals and tours are available at numerous sites throughout the spring, summer and fall.

DO IT IF: You wish to view Boston and Cambridge from a river perspective.

SKIP IT IF: The Charles River frightens you.

LOCAL ADVICE: Because the river flows through numerous neighborhoods on both sides there are multiple locations where you can launch from making the Charles River very accessible.

I DID IT: ☐ Paddleboston.com

DID YOU KNOW?

Canoe, kayak, and paddleboarders with their own equipment can launch from several locations, though the three launch locations with easy accessiblity and parking are Magazine Beach, Herter Park, and the MDC boat ramp between Day Field and Community Rowing.

5

WATCH THE FIREWORKS FROM THE HATCH SHELL

WHAT'S THE DEAL?   The hatch shell along the esplanade of the Charles River and location of the Boston Pops concert is probably the most iconic spot to watch the 4th of July fireworks display. Boston is renowned for offering one of the most celebrated fireworks exhibitions in the country.

DO IT IF: You want a front row seat to the 4th of July festivities!

SKIP IT IF: You don't like crowds or traffic. Some years a half a million people line the riverside to see the show.

LOCAL ADVICE: Soon after the concert ends, the Boston fireworks begin to be launched from 7 barges in the middle of the Charles River. The show lasts about 20 minutes and concludes at 11pm. If you wish to watch from home, many local stations synchronize the fireworks show to music for your viewing pleasure.

I DID IT: ☐   www.boston-discovery-guide.com/boston-fireworks

DID YOU KNOW?

The concert on July 4th is part of a fabulous show including a fighter jet military flyover and a terrific lineup of special guests and finishing with fireworks.The music is terrific, and then comes the finale -Tchaikovsky's explosive 1812 Overture, ending with dramatic drumrolls and real cannon fire, while church bells ring throughout the city.

FIND THE GRAVE OF MOTHER GOOSE

WHAT'S THE DEAL? Mary Goose was a real person, living in the colony of Boston and dying in the year 1690. The gravestone can be found in the Granary Burying Ground along the freedom trail.

DO IT IF: You wish to pay your respects to a great storyteller.

SKIP IT IF: Graveyards frighten you.

LOCAL ADVICE: Take a few minutes and stroll around the Granary Burying ground. Not only will you see Mary "Mother" Goose's stone, but see many other famous names like Franklin, Hancock and Adams.

I DID IT:

DID YOU KNOW?

This grave in an old Boston cemetery is promoted to tourists as Mother Goose's burial site -- the 1690 tombstone of Mary Goose, first wife of Isaac Goose. His second wife, the Mother Goose who is said to have actually inspired the fictional character might be buried here too, but no one is sure.

7

WALK THROUGH THE GATES OF HARVARD

WHAT'S THE DEAL? Take a stroll through the gates of one of the world's most famous and influential educational institutions. Just walking around the campus, you will not only see students from all over the world, but enjoy centuries of amazing architecture as well, dating back to 1636.

DO IT IF: You want to walk around the hallowed halls of Harvard.

SKIP IT IF: Ivy League institutions offend you sense of reality.

LOCAL ADVICE: You can ride the red line to Harvard Square walk the campus and enjoy the neighborhood. You will find great local restaurants, corner coffee shops and eclectic bookstores surrounding the historic campus.

I DID IT: ☐   Harvard.edu

DID YOU KNOW?

While on campus you may hear someone to recommend you touch the foot of the John Harvard statue for good luck. We would strongly advise against touching the object in any way. Harvard pranksters are notorious for relieving themselves on that lucky foot, after a night of reveling.

TAKE THE FERRY TO BOSTON LIGHT

WHAT'S THE DEAL? Located about 9 miles east of downtown Boston on Little Brewster Island, the current lighthouse was constructed in 1783. Access to the island is limited due to the fact it is one of only 5 coast guard manned light stations remaining. Limited tours are available by prior reservation.

DO IT IF: You want to explore America's oldest lighthouse.

SKIP IT IF: You have limited time, the ferry ride and tour can be time consuming, especially with limited ferry service.

LOCAL ADVICE: If you have limited time or the Lighthouse is not available due to weather conditions or maintenance, you might want to consider a harbor cruise past the lighthouse instead. The 2 hour tours depart from Long Wharf behind the Marriott near the entrance to the Aquarium.

I DID IT: ☐   www.bostonharborislands.org/tour-lighthouse

DID YOU KNOW?

Boston Light is a lighthouse located on Little Brewster Island in outer Boston Harbor. The first lighthouse to be built on the site dates back to 1716. The current lighthouse dates from 1783, is the second oldest working lighthouse in the United States (after Sandy Hook Lighthouse in New Jersey), and is the only lighthouse to still be actively staffed by the United States Coast Guard.

FEAST AT THE FOOD COURT

WHAT'S THE DEAL? Quincy Market's food court features over 30 dining options featuring some of Boston's most famous restaurants and cuisines. Whether you crave hot dogs, pizza, chowda or Chinese, you'll find it all under one roof.

DO IT IF: You want to sample all the amazing foods Boston offers in one convenient location.

SKIP IT IF: Eating in a sometimes frantic, crowded environment or even standing up when seating options aren't available.

LOCAL ADVICE: If you want a couple places to try, we have a couple of favorites for you. The corned beef and cabbage eggrolls at Ned Devine's, a cup of chowda at the Boston Chowder company or the Boston baked beans at cheers will get you off to a good start. Make sure you save room for dessert!

I DID IT: ☐ www.faneuilhallmarketplace.com/restaurants

DID YOU KNOW?

Opened in 1743, it was the site of several speeches by Samuel Adams, James Otis, and others encouraging independence from Great Britain. It is now part of Boston National Historical Park and a well-known stop on the Freedom Trail. It is sometimes referred to as "the Cradle of Liberty"

10

TOUR BY LAND AND SEA

What's the deal?

The Boston Duck tour began in 1994 using World War II surplus amphibious vehicles. These unique craft allow you to see Boston's historic sites from land. Then the Duck Boats plunge into the Charles River, providing an unforgettable view while winding through the city's famous waterway.

Do it if: Exploring 2 different perspectives of the same city excites you.

Skip it if: Amphibious vehicles rolling through the narrow Boston streets seems antithetical.

Local Advice: Locals and tourists alike always enjoy the Boston Duck boat tours. Many guides are local actors and comedians, so their performances always evolve with new highlights and no two tours are every the same. And if you are nice to the guide/driver, they may even let you steer the duck while on the Charles.

I DID IT: ☐   Bostonducktours.com

DID YOU KNOW?

The company started running tours in Boston with four Ducks and now runs a fleet of 28. As of 2015 all regular tours are conducted on replica DUCKs that are larger and easier to repair than the original vehicles, and run on bio diesel.

11

MIKES OR MODERN?

WHAT'S THE DEAL? While walking through the Boston streets, you will notice people carrying white paper boxes, neatly tied with string. People in the know, know these boxes contain some of Boston's most coveted items! Desserts from the North End's favorite confection shops. Italian cookies, éclairs and of course one of Boston's personal favorite, Cannoli's.

DO IT IF: You crave sweets from an authentic Italian bakery.

SKIP IT IF: You are dieting.

LOCAL ADVICE: Our personal favorite is the Cannoli with the Florentine shell at Mike's pastries with ricotta filing, topped with powdered sugar and capped with chocolate chips. But try Mikes and Modern pastries on Hanover Street and decide for yourself. Trust us, it is an age-old argument! Honestly, they are both delicious!

I DID IT: ☐   www.mikespastry.com
www.modernpastry.com

DID YOU KNOW?

Cannoli are Italian pastries consisting of tube-shaped shells of fried pastry dough, filled with a sweet, creamy filling usually containing ricotta—a staple of Sicilian cuisine. The true Italian versions are made with ricotta, not vanilla or Boston cream.

12

DON'T FIRE TILL YOU SEE THE WHITES OF THEIR EYES

WHAT'S THE DEAL? This famous statement was uttered by an unknown commander during the Battle of Bunker Hill, June 17th, 1775. (Although much of the battle was on nearby Breed's Hill.) It was one of the first battles of the American Revolution and there were heavy casualties on both sides. Dozens of British Officers as well as Dr. Joseph Warren, President of the Massachusetts provincial congress, perishing during this hill side skirmish.

DO IT IF: You are trying to explore Boston's revolutionary war sites.

SKIP IT IF: Urban battlefields are offensive to your peaceful nature.

LOCAL ADVICE: Not only can you see one of the most important battlefields of the American revolution, but you can also enjoy the grassy hillside and even climb the Bunker Hill monument. From the top you will have amazing views of Boston Harbor and the city skyline.

I DID IT: ☐ www.nps.gov/bost/learn/historyculture

DID YOU KNOW?

The Battle of Bunker Hill was fought on June 17, 1775, during the early stages of the American Revolution. The battle is named after Bunker Hill in Charlestown, Massachusetts, which was peripherally involved in the battle. It was the original objective of both the colonial and British troops, though the major fighting took place next to it on Breed's Hill.

13

COME FACE TO FACE WITH A SHARK

WHAT'S THE DEAL?   The New England Aquarium has one of the most complete and comprehensive collections of sea life in the world. One of the newest attractions is the penguin exhibit featuring the secret life of these enigmatic birds. Another highlight of the aquarium is the 4 story, 200,000 gallon salt water tank featuring Caribbean Sea life including sea turtles, stingrays, and eels. And don't forget the touch tank, where you can get up close and personal with a shark.

DO IT IF: The under sea world is fascinating to you.

SKIP IT IF: Viewing live fish and sea creatures in their natural habitat bores you.

LOCAL ADVICE: Take your time and walk around the winding ramp, encircling the giant 4 story central tank. You will be mesmerized by the natural beauty of the coral reef and the variety of fish living harmoniously in the windowed eco-system. Check the feeding times when you arrive so you can watch the diver hand feed the sharks.

I DID IT: ☐   Neaq.org

DID YOU KNOW?

The star of the exhibit is Myrtle the green sea turtle. She has lived at the Aquarium since June 1970, and many adult visitors remember seeing her when they came to the Aquarium as children. Myrtle shares the Giant Ocean Tank with about 1,000 animals. I remember Myrtle the turtle from my first visit in 1975.

14

STROLL NEWBURY STREET

WHAT'S THE DEAL? Newbury Street is Boston's most fashionable shopping district and was originally part of the harbor. In the late 1850's this area was slowly filled in and was finally completed in 1882. Now known as the Rodeo Drive of the East, these tony 8 blocks are filled with upscale boutiques, fine dining restaurants and stylish salons.

DO IT IF: Your shopping budget has no limits.

SKIP IT IF: Your style is more Filene's basement.

LOCAL ADVICE: On the east end closer to Boston Common, you will find Tiffany & Co, Cartier, Valentino, rag & bone, Jack Wills, Woolrich, Steven Alan, Zara, Urban Outfitters, Lady M, Uniqlo and Muji make up the diverse retail landscape. More recently, the shopping street has become a popular destination for highly produced pop up shops. Many e-commerce brands use temporary storefronts on Newbury Street to test the Boston market for expansion, often landing as permanent fixtures on the retail strip.

I DID IT: ☐ www.newburystboston.com

DID YOU KNOW?

Newbury Comics began as a comic book vendor on Newbury Street.The company was founded in 1978 by 2 MIT students.Over the next few years, the focus of the company changed from comics to music, although comic books are still sold at stores in limited quantities.

15

SKATE THE FROG POND

WHAT'S THE DEAL? The Boston Common reflecting pool has a different role   in the winter, becoming a skating rink. Located in the oldest public park in the United States, the rink offers lessons, rentals and a café to buy some hot chocolate.

DO IT IF: You enjoy a fun winter activity in a park like setting.

SKIP IT IF: You get cold easily.

LOCAL ADVICE: Sorry, no hockey allowed Happy Gilmore, but they will rent you hockey or figure skates, it is your call. But bring a helmet just to play it safe. Locker rentals are available to store your gear and skating lessons are also available for beginners.

I DID IT: ☐ Bostonfrogpond.com

DID YOU KNOW?

Although the frogs are gone, the skating area was once a shallow pond on the common. The city-maintained rink provides its own ice making and cooling system if mother nature doesn't make it cold enough for perfect ice.

16

SEE THE SPOT OF THE BOSTON MASSACRE

WHAT'S THE DEAL?   Just below the balcony of the Old State House, the Incident on King Street occurred, March 5, 1770. A crowd had gathered and was antagonizing the British soldiers standing guard by throwing snowballs and rocks. Eventually the troops fired their muskets to subdue the crowd and killed 5 bystanders, resulting in one of the first sparks of the American Revolution.

DO IT IF: You are on a mission to see all of the city's Revolutionary War sites.

SKIP IT IF: You are not revolutionary.

LOCAL ADVICE: A snowball fight between locals and British soldiers escalated into an armed confrontation. Look for the circle of bricks just below the balcony to see the actual location of the massacre. The Sons of Liberty held funerals for the victims and organized a vigorous propaganda effort in order to turn public opinion against the Redcoats and labeled the tragedy a "bloody massacre." The first victim was an African American dockworker named Crispus Attucks and was buried in the Granary Burying Ground.

I DID IT: nps.gov/places/boston-massacre-site.

DID YOU KNOW?

Boston attorney and future U.S. president John Adams defended the 9 British Soldiers accused of killing innocent civilians in the Massacre. Adams felt it was his duty to ensure they received a fair trial, and they were acquitted when Adamas raised the reasonable defense argument, the first time it was used in a trial.

17

TAKE THE FOOD CHALLENGE AT EAGLE'S DELI

WHAT'S THE DEAL? Are you a big eater, with a healthy appetite? Well then, you should head over to Eagle's Deli in Cleveland circle and take on their food challenge. The Eagle's challenge is 6lbs of burger, 24pcs of bacon, 24pcs of American cheese, 5lbs of fries, and 1 deli pickle. If you eat it all in 1 hour it's free, if you fail it will set you back $69.99. Good Luck!

DO IT IF: You are a glutton or practicing for the hot dog eating challenge.

SKIP IT IF: You are a vegetarian.

LOCAL ADVICE: Bring a big appetite if you are planning to challenge the Eagle's deli. If you succeed you get a T-Shirt, your photo on the wall of fame and perhaps heartburn. The Deli also has a good breakfast menu and reasonably priced sandwiches as well if you aren't trying to stuff yourself.

I DID IT: ☐ Eaglesdeli.com

DID YOU KNOW?

Adam Richmond of Man vs. Food attempted the challenge in 2009 and lost. Up to that point 1500 people had tried and no one had succeeded, although recently a handful of participants have finally broken through and defeated the giant burger.

18

FIND JOHN HANCOCK'S HAND

WHAT'S THE DEAL? John Hancock, the man with the large and famous signature on the declaration of independence was buried in Boston's granary burying ground in 1793. As one of Boston's wealthiest and most prominent citizens, Hancock was buried with his signature ruby rings. Grave robbers knew this as well and quickly attempted to remove the rings shortly after Hancock's demise. Because the famous signers' fingers had swelled after death, the robbers just cut off the hand, rings and all and disappeared into the Boston night!

DO IT IF: You interested in solving an old mystery.

SKIP IT IF: You don't care about the missing hand.

LOCAL ADVICE: Another reason to tour the Granary Burying ground is to see the final resting place of some of Boston's most prominent early citizens and 2 other signers of the Declaration of Independence. Even though many are not even still buried there anymore.

I DID IT: ☐ www.thefreedomtrail.org/trail-sites/granary-burying ground

DID YOU KNOW?

When the church on the west side of the Burying Ground was expanded, the body of John Hancock was removed for a later burial after the renovations were completed. But the remains were mis places and never re interred, so there is no body under the massive Hancock tombstone.

19

HAVE A DRINK WHERE EVERYONE KNOWS YOUR NAME

WHAT'S THE DEAL? If you remember the famous 1980's TV show Cheers, you will remember their jingle. The TV show was based on a Beacon Hill Bar called the Bull and Finch. Stop by and reminisce about Norm, Cliff, Coach, Diane, Sam, Woody and the rest of the gang.

DO IT IF: You want everyone to know your name.

SKIP IT IF: You were more of a Frasier fan.

LOCAL ADVICE: Even if you are not a big drinker, walking into the bar is like a trip down memory lane. Only a short walk from Boston common and across from the public garden, the setting is just like you will remember form the mega popular 1980's show.

I DID IT: ☐ Cheersboston.com

DID YOU KNOW?

When the producers of the TV show went looking for a location to depict the ideal American bar, they headed to Boston, famous for colorful pubs, sports teams, and lively politics.

20

DRINK FROM PAUL REVERE'S TANKARD

WHAT'S THE DEAL? Not only was Paul Revere a noted son of liberty he was also a well-respected silversmith. He was ahead of his time, even using silver to fill cavities for fellow Bostonians. A silver tankard or spoon from this noted silversmith would be a prized possession in any era. You can still tour the Revere house along the freedom trail as well.

DO IT IF: You enjoy exploring houses of famous American Patriots.

DO IT IF: You enjoy exploring houses of famous American Patriots.

SKIP IT IF: Perhaps you feel Revere was a traitor to the crown.

LOCAL ADVICE: The Revere house remains Boston's oldest private residence and is a noted site along the freedom trail. Originally built in 1680 by a local minister, Revere and his family owned the property from 1770 until 1800.

I DID IT: ☐ Paulreverhouse.org

DID YOU KNOW?

Paul Revere opened the first successful copper rolling mill in North America in 1801. He provided copper sheeting for the hull of USS Constitution when it was re-coppered and the dome of the new Massachusetts State House in 1802. He is also known for "Revere Ware" copper-bottomed pots and pans.

21

DISCOVER THE TREASURES OF THE MUSEUM OF FINE ARTS

WHAT'S THE DEAL? Located on Huntington Avenue, the MFA as it is known locally is one of the largest museums in the country. The museum features a permanent collection of ancient artifacts, contemporary art and even photography. They also feature rotating exhibits that make this a must-see attraction.

DO IT IF: You enjoy all aspects of art in 1 convenient location from all over the world.

SKIP IT IF: Art is a guy you knew from grade school.

LOCAL ADVICE: The Art of the Americas collection includes more than 2,000 paintings created throughout the United States, Canada, and Latin America, ranging from the colonial period through the mid-20th century. Many have become icons of American art, among them John Singleton Copley's portrait of Paul Revere, Mary Cassatt's In the Loge and Winslow Homer's the Fog Warning. There is also a small selection also includes 19th-century landscapes and important modernist and abstract works by Georgia O'Keeffe, Jackson Pollock and Norman Lewis.

I DID IT: ☐   www.mfa.org

DID YOU KNOW?

The Museum of Fine Arts is the 14th largest art museum in the world, measured by public gallery area. It contains more than 450,000 works of art, making it one of the most comprehensive collections in the Americas. It is home to 8,161 paintings, surpassed only by the Metropolitan Museum of Art in New York City.

22

SAMPLE SUDS AT THE SAM ADAMS BREWERY

WHAT'S THE DEAL? The Sam Adams Brewery located south of downtown offers 1-hour tours of the entire brewing process. The Boston Brewing company gift shop even offers seasonal beers for sale by the bottle or even by the growler. The tour is by donation and the proceeds benefit local charities.

DO IT IF: You want to see one of the original craft breweries up close and personal.

DO IT IF: You want to see one of the original craft breweries up close and personal.

SKIP IT IF: You prefer vineyards.

LOCAL ADVICE: Jim Koch brewed the first batch of Boston Lager in his kitchen – a recipe that belonged to his great great grandfather that he found in his father's attic back in the early 1980's. The brewery has grown over the years and brews dozens of beers as well as seasonal selections. Check out the Taproom at the Brewery to sample the freshest beer in Boston.

I DID IT: ☐ www.samadams.com

DID YOU KNOW?

Jim Koch started Sam Adams in his kitchen in 1984, when imports and mass domestics were the only option for beer lovers. In turn, he ignited a revolution, the craft beer movement, inspiring a whole new category that's produced millions of jobs in communities from coast-to-coast.

23

SAIL A SCHOONER

WHAT'S THE DEAL? One of the best ways to see the modern skyline as well as some of the historic sites along the Boston Waterfront is to sail on a historic schooner. The Liberty Fleet is one of the more popular options, which sails seasonally from when the weather is conducive to be on the harbor.

DO IT IF: You enjoy a boat ride with the wind through the sails.

SKIP IT IF: You are a power boat person.

LOCAL ADVICE: Come aboard for a day sail in Boston on one of their classic schooners with plenty of deck space well as lots of fresh air and sunshine! The 2-hour sail aboard the Liberty Clipper is a great, family-friendly way to see Boston from a new viewpoint. Get away from the hustle and bustle of city streets and enjoy some quality time with family or friends. You can also learn more about Boston with some of our captain and crew's interesting and informative commentary as we sail. There is a cash bar on board if you need an adult beverage and bring a light jacket or sweatshirt because its typically cooler on the harbor.

I DID IT: ☐ www.libertyfleet.com/boston-sailing

DID YOU KNOW?

Before Boston was a walking city, it was an active seaport. For most of Boston's history, the harbor was the center of the city, and urban life was dominated by sailing ships. The city was the crown jewel of the Brisitish empire and one of the 5 busiest colonial seaport along with New York,Philadelphia, Newport,Rhode Island and Charleston, South Carolina.

24

USE A SKYSCRAPER TO PREDICT THE WEATHER

WHAT'S THE DEAL? Kids these days and their fancy cell phones. In the olden days before the internet, the Berkeley Building, o The Old John Hancock Building. Used various lighting sequences to tell Bostonians the weather.

DO IT IF: You long for the days of nostalgic weather telling, before you could just glance at the phone.

SKIP IT IF: It is only modern conveniences for you.

LOCAL ADVICE: I remember on various trips to Boston to visit family, my father would always reminisce about the old skyline of Boston. This of course was in the 1970's when the Prudential Center and John Hancock Building dominated the city center. The Berkeley Building was Boston's 2nd highest tower until 1964 but old-time residents knew the tower for another reason. The beacon was first lit on March 15, 1950 and was controlled using forecasts from a meteorological agency located on the 26th floor. If it flashed red, it meant the Red Sox game was rained out.

I DID IT:

DID YOU KNOW?

Bostonians learned the forecast by these ryhmes, based on the lights. Steady blue, clear view,Flashing blue, clouds due. Steady red, rain ahead,Flashing red, snow instead. In 2004 when the Red Sox finally won the world series a new line was added: Flashing Blue and Red, when The Curse of the Bambino is dead!

25

SPEND THE DAY AT A PRESIDENTIAL LIBRARY

WHAT'S THE DEAL? The John F. Kennedy presidential library is a must see for any fans of American or presidential history. Located just south of downtown, in the Dorchester neighborhood, the library features the 35th president's personal items, official white house photos and papers as well as unique items from many Kennedy family members.

DO IT IF: You live for Camelot and cherish the Kennedy clan.

SKIP IT IF: Presidential libraries are not for you.

LOCAL ADVICE: After years of delays, the JFK presidential library opened its doors in 1979. The Presidential Library and Museum is dedicated to the memory of our nation's thirty-fifth president and to all those who through the art of politics seek a new and better world. Located on a ten-acre park, overlooking the sea that he loved and the city that launched him to greatness, the Library stands as a tribute to the life and times of the former president. Researchers and students can also make an appointment to search the library's archives to delve into JFK's letter and personal documents.

I DID IT: ☐ Jfklibrary.org

DID YOU KNOW?

Sadly, 1 month before his untimely death, President Kennedy chose a location next to Harvard University in Cambridge, to construct his Presidential library and office where he could conduct personal business after his time in office. Fund raising and construction delays hindered the opening for more than 15 years before the library was finally completed in 1979.

26

RIDE A SWAN

WHAT'S THE DEAL? One of the most iconic symbols of Boston, the swan boats have cruised around a pond at the public garden since 1877. The boat ride lasts about 15 minutes and the boat's pilot powers the ride by pedaling, which turns a small paddle wheel to peacefully propel your swan. The swan boats operate from April to September.

DO IT IF: You are looking for a unique way to spend time on the water.

SKIP IT IF: You are tentative about someone padding you around a pond on a bird.

LOCAL ADVICE: You really can't beat the price, to experience a Boston tradition passed on for generations. The rides last up to 15 minutes but the memories will last a lifetime. No reservations are need so even if there is a long line to enter, it moves quickly because each swan can take a large number of guests.

I DID IT: ☐ www.swanboats.com

DID YOU KNOW?

Robert Paget first created the Swan Boats in the Public Garden in 1877, after seeing the opera Lohengrin with his wife Julia. Inspired by the knight's gallant rescue of the damsel by riding a swan across the lake, Paget decided to capitalize on the recent popularity of the bicycle and combine the two. Its been a cultural icon ever since.

27

VISIT THE SPOT OF THE SHOT HEARD ROUND THE WORLD

WHAT'S THE DEAL? Historians disagree on the actual location of the first shots fired against British occupation, but many locals will argue they took place at the North Bridge in Concord. Nearby Lexington also claims to have fired the first shots of resistance, so in a world of political correctness, visit both of these charming historic towns.

DO IT IF: You are visiting all the important Revolutionary War sites around Boston.

SKIP IT IF: You are short on time, it is about 30 minutes northwest of downtown.

LOCAL ADVICE: If you do make the trip, a must see is the nearly 1,000 acres across Lincoln, Lexington and Concord, Minute Man National Historical Park. It features a wealth of rich landmarks associated with the American Revolution. Perhaps the most prominent, North Bridge is the site of the romanticized "shot heard 'round the world" of April 19, 1775. If you want to see 2 quintessential New England towns, Lexington and Concord are a great choice, especially in the fall with the colorful autumn leaves.

I DID IT: ☐   www.nps.gov/mima

DID YOU KNOW?

On the night of April 18, 1775, hundreds of British troops marched from Boston to nearby Concord in order to seize an arms cache. Paul Revere and other riders sounded the alarm, and colonial militiamen began mobilizing to intercept the Redcoat column. A confrontation on the Lexington town green started off the fighting, and soon the British were hastily retreating under intense fire.

28

TOUCH LIGHTNING

WHAT'S THE DEAL? The museum of science is truly a Boston landmark, with over 700 different exhibits. The multiple wings include a planetarium, a domed Imax theatre, over 100 live animals and a visitor's favorite; the world's largest Van de Graaff generator producing artificial lightning.

DO IT IF: Science!

SKIP IT IF: You are a science denier.

LOCAL ADVICE: As a high school student our class took a field trip to the Museum of Science and a couple things still stick with me from that visit. One was the complete skeleton of a triceratops. Another lasting memory was the full-size model of a T-Rex which continues to be updated when new bones are unearthed. By far my favorite exhibit was the Van de Graaff generator, which produces indoor lightning. There are more than 30 permanent exhibits, planetarium shows, live presentations and 4-D films so try to spend a day at least exploring the museum.

I DID IT: ☐ www.mos.org

DID YOU KNOW?

The museum is also an accredited member of the Association of Zoos and Aquariums and is home to over 100 animals, many of which have been rescued and rehabilitated. There is even a butterfly garden which features a walk through greenhouse featuring the exotic creatures.

29

RIDE THE RED LINE

WHAT'S THE DEAL? One of the best ways to get around the crowded inner city of Boston is to ride the MBTA of locally called the "T" This 5-line rail system conveniently travels to most of the city's important cultural, business and historic attractions. Day passes can be purchased at each station and the T will zip you around so you can complete your bucket list.

DO IT IF: You want to avoid traffic while visiting multiple spots around Boston.

SKIP IT IF: You prefer to take your car.

LOCAL ADVICE: If you are day tripping to downtown Boston, the "T" might be a good option for you. Park in the commuter garage at the Quincy Adams stop and purchase your Charlie pass for unlimited rides for the day. You'll avoid Boston traffic and trying to find an overpriced parking spot. The red line can take you to Boston common, the JFK library, MIT and Harvard in Cambridge.

I DID IT: ☐   Mbta.com

DID YOU KNOW?

Opened in September 1897, the four-track-wide segment of the Green Line tunnel between Park Street and Boylston stations was the first subway in the United States, and has been designated a National Historic Landmark. Streetcar congestion in downtown Boston led to the establishment of subways and elevated rail stations throughout the city.

30

CATCH A GAME AT THE TD GARDEN

WHAT'S THE DEAL? The TD Garden, built in 1995, replaced the aging but legendary Boston Garden. Currently the home of the Basketball Celtics and the Hockey Bruins, Boston fans are known to be among the most passionate sports fan in the country.

DO IT IF: You are a big NBA or NHL fan or you love live sports.

SKIP IT IF: You swore you would never see a game in person if they tore down the old "Gaardehn."

LOCAL ADVICE: For a true Boston sports experience, arrive early and have a few beers or grab a pre-game snack at on the many bars along Causeway Street just steps from the arena. But a word of caution. Boston sports fans are very territorial about their teams, especially Bruin's fans. So, we don't recommend wearing a Montreal Canadiens Jersey to The Harp or West End Johnnies.

I DID IT: ☐ Tdgarden.com

DID YOU KNOW?

Located on the 5th and 6th floors of the TD Garden is the Sports Museum, a must visit for true Boston sports fans. The museum's exhibits focus on the history of various sports in the area, including the Boston Bruins, the Boston Celtics, the New England Patriots, the Boston Red Sox and many more.

31

WATCH A WATERFRONT CONCERT

WHAT'S THE DEAL? Now called the Rockland Trust Bank pavilion, this 5000 seat amphitheater has hosted some of Boston's most memorable waterfront concerts. Located on the South Boston Waterfront, adjacent to Rowes Wharf, enjoy the downtown view and the live music from May to September.

DO IT IF: You live for live music in a cozy outdoor setting.

SKIP IT IF: You need a stadium experience to attend a concert.

LOCAL ADVICE: Although the naming rights have changed over the years, the music has been consistent at this seaport district location since 1999. I actually saw a Bare-Naked Ladies here in 2013 and was one of the best concerts I have ever attended. The small size of the venue with Boston Harbor as the backdrop just added to the ambiance.

I DID IT: ☐ livenation.com

DID YOU KNOW?

The venue originally opened August 1994 near Fan Pier and was originally called the Harborlights pavillion.Due to land rights, the venue closed at the end of its season in 1998 and was relocated to its current location in South Boston, in 1999.

32

AVOID MOLASSES

WHAT'S THE DEAL? One of the most tragic and bizarre events to place in Boston happened on January 15, 1919 in the North End. A giant holding tank exploded and a wave of more than 2 million gallons of the sticky, sweet mixture poured onto the street at an amazing 35 miles per hour. The flood trapped 21 victims and injured 150. Local folklore even says on hot summer days, you can still smell the remnants of the molasses flood in the air.

DO IT IF: You wish to avoid a wave of a sticky demise.

SKIP IT IF: You seek a bizarre way to perish.

LOCAL ADVICE: This is a nice scenic area to walk around now, it has been re-developed since it earlier industrial days. It is now the site of a city-owned recreational complex, officially named Langone Park, featuring a Little League Baseball field, a playground, and bocce courts. Directly to the east is the larger Puopolo Park, with addition recreational facilities.

I DID IT: ☐   www.history.com/news/great-molasses-flood-science

DID YOU KNOW?

Rescue workers, cleanup crews, and sight-seers had tracked molasses through the streets and spread it to subway platforms, to the seats inside trains and streetcars, to pay telephone handsets, into homes and numerous other places. Everything that Bostonians touched was sticky for months after the disaster.

33

EAT BOSTON CREAM PIE

WHAT'S THE DEAL? You can eat Boston cream pie at the very place it was invented! It was first made at the Parker House Hotel in 1856 and originally called Parker House chocolate cream pie. For those who have never tried this delicious confection, it is a 2-layer sponge cake with a layer of custard inside and topped with chocolate.

DO IT IF: You want to sample the official dessert of Massachusetts.

SKIP IT IF: You prefer German Chocolate Cake.

LOCAL ADVICE: If you are Boston, then dine where the famous pie got its start, right inside the elegant Parker Restaurant. If you want to try the original, the restaurant will ship you one anywhere across the country. The original Boston Cream Pie prepared fresh and shipped directly from the bake shop right to your door. Each original Boston Cream pie is 8 inches in diameter, 44 oz. and contains nuts. Serves 10 to 12 people.

I DID IT: ☐ www.omnihotels.com/hotels/boston-parker-house

DID YOU KNOW?

The current hotel on the site, the Omni Parker Hotel, was built in 1927 and has had its share of famous guests. John F. Kennedy announced his candidacy for Congress in 1946 and also held his bachelor party in the hotel's Press Room there in 1953.Charles Dickens lived there for 2 years, Ho Chi Minh toiled as a baker and Malcolm X worked as a bellman.

34

VISIT OLD IRONSIDES

WHAT'S THE DEAL? The U.S.S Constitution is the oldest naval vessel afloat. Launched in 1797, the Constitution first saw action against the Barbary Pirates of the coast of Africa. She received her famous nickname while fighting the British during the War of 1812.

DO IT IF: Your motto is "Go Navy!"

SKIP IT IF: You prefer to see modern warships.

LOCAL ADVICE: Truly one of America's great warships, the U.S.S Constitution is synonymous with Boston. Tours of Constitution are self-paced and with the top three decks open to the public. The fully commissioned Naval Vessel is staffed by active personal with a mission of education and participation in public events and ceremonies.

I DID IT: ☐ www.nps.gov/bost/learn/historyculture/ussconst.htm

DID YOU KNOW?

The sturdily built war ship had British cannonballs bouncing off her side, earning the vessel the nickname, "Old Ironsides." The historic ship is currently berthed at the Charlestown Navy yard on the freedom trail and is open year-round for tours.

35

SIT WITH RED

WHAT'S THE DEAL?   The legendary coach and general manager of the Boston Celtics, Arnold "Red" Auerbach, won 16 titles in 29 years, making him one of the immortals in basketball history. His status as a sports icon was galvanized when his statue was placed outside of Quincy Market.

DO IT IF: You bleed Celtic's Green.

SKIP IT IF: You are a Laker fan.

LOCAL ADVICE: Located on the south side of Quincy Market there is a spot on the bench next to the legendary coach for you to have a seat. Red is a good listener if you have something to get off your chest. If Coach Auerbach responds, there is either a ventriloquist close by, or you have a few too many Bud Lights.

I DID IT: ☐   faneuilhallmarketplace.com

DID YOU KNOW?

Auerbach was known for his love for cigar smoking. Because the legendary coach made his victory cigars a tradition in the 1960s, Boston restaurants would often say "no cigar or pipe smoking, "except for Red Auerbach.

36

TOUR BOSTON'S OLDEST HOUSE

WHAT'S THE DEAL? The James Blake House, built in 1661, is the oldest remaining colonial house and is located in the Boston neighborhood of Dorchester. Now owned by the Dorchester historical society, tours are given on the 3rd Sunday of each month.

DO IT IF: You enjoy visiting living history.

SKIP IT IF: You don't find old homes appealing.

LOCAL ADVICE: As the oldest house in the Boston area, it is certainly worth a visit if you are a fan of touring colonial homes. But keep in mind it is only tourable 1 day a month, so plan accordingly.

I DID IT: www.dorchesterhistoricalsociety.org

DID YOU KNOW?

The house was built in a Western English style of post-medieval architecture by James Blake, an immigrant from England. The Blake family owned the house until 1825. In order to save the house from demolition in 1896, the Dorchester Historical Society acquired the property from the City and moved the house less than 500 feet from its original location

37

FORAGE AT A FARMERS MARKET

WHAT'S THE DEAL? The Boston Public Market is an indoor, year-round marketplace featuring about 30 New England artisans and food producers housed under one roof offering fresh foods, prepared meals, crafts, and specialty items.

DO IT IF: You prefer fresh organic food grown locally.

SKIP IT IF: You don't want to support local growers or prefer processed foods.

LOCAL ADVICE: Residents and visitors alike can find seasonal, locally sourced food from Massachusetts and New England, including fresh produce, meat and poultry, eggs, dairy, seafood, baked goods, specialty items, crafts, and prepared breakfast, lunch, and dinner options. Everything sold at the Market is produced or originates in New England, as the seasons allow.

I DID IT: ☐ bostonpublicmarket.org

DID YOU KNOW?

In 2001, the Boston Public Market Association was formed by a dedicated coalition of food lovers, food producers, and state and city officials. After years of work advocating for the development of a public market in Boston. In 2011, state and city officials settled on a location for the market on the Rose Fitzgerald Kennedy Greenway, directly above the Haymarket MBTA

38

VISIT THE OLD COUNTRY

WHAT'S THE DEAL? Boston has for a long time attracted immigrants to its various neighborhoods. This of course it reflected in the different types of foods and cuisines available throughout the city. The north end has for generations attracted Italian residents. The south side of Boston was predominantly Irish. Recently the east side of the city has been attracting a Latin crowd. Boston also has an exceptionally large Asian population found predominantly in China Town. Recently, along Massachusetts Avenue to Central Square, numerous Middle Eastern restaurants have sprung up, reflecting an influx from that part of the world.

DO IT IF: You wish to visit many countries all within 1 city.

SKIP IT IF: You suffer from xenophobia.

LOCAL ADVICE: As a descendant of an Irish-Italian family from Cambridge I am certainly familiar with the melting plot of greater Boston. My personal favorite would be the North End neighborhood, the authentic Italian food, desserts and the colorful characters on almost every corner.

I DID IT: ☐ brewminate.com/a-history-of-immigration-to-boston-eras -ethnic-groups-and-places

DID YOU KNOW?

In greater Boston, recent immigrants have come from a strikingly diverse array of countries, mainly in Asia, Latin America, and the Caribbean. China, Haiti and the Dominican Republic have long been the top countries of origin, but sizeable groups also hail from Brazil, India, Vietnam, El Salvador, and Guatemala.

39

DINE OVERLOOKING THE HARBOR

WHAT'S THE DEAL? Some of Boston's most amazing harbor views are from waterfront restaurants surrounding the waterfront. Whether you try Strega waterfront, Rowe's wharf seafood, The Charthouse, Yankees Lobster Fish Market or Sam's, these highly rated restaurants offer great cuisine with water views.

DO IT IF: You wish to create a memorable dining experience with amazing views.

SKIP IT IF: The view is not for you, Its just about the FOOD!

LOCAL ADVICE: Growing up near Boston, Anthony's Pier 4 was always the go to spot for waterfront dining. The restaurant is gone but a new concept has taken its place with the same harborside views.

I DID IT: ☐   www.woodshillpier4.com

DID YOU KNOW?

Woods Hill Pier 4 brings farm-to-table dining to the Seaport, on the site where the iconic Anthony's Pier 4 restaurant once sat. The team behind The Farm at Woods Hill create modern, seasonal dishes using ingredients that are organic and come from local area purveyors.

40

STUMBLE OUT OF THE BEER WORKS

WHAT'S THE DEAL? With various locations throughout the city, the Boston Beer works features dozens of craft and specialty beers with a rotating seasonal menu.

DO IT IF: You like friendly, well-lit modern large beer halls that serve dozens of tap beers.

SKIP IT IF: You prefer poorly lit, dank, seedy corner taverns.

LOCAL ADVICE: As you can tell, Bostonians love their beer. The beer works are located throughout the Boston area and one of the most popular location is the one close to Fenway Park. It's a great spot to grab a pre-game meal and a couple brews before heading to the park.

I DID IT: ☐ www.beerworks.com

DID YOU KNOW?

Not only does the beer works offer dozens of tap beers they have a sizeable menu as well. They provide what they call New England Comfort Food which are classics and some newer dishes. Cooked to order and made from scratch. Sizeable portions and reasonable prices, especially for Boston!

41

GOOD WILL HUNTING

WHAT'S THE DEAL? If you are a fan of the 1997 movie featuring local boys Matt Damon, Ben Affleck and the now deceased Robin Williams, there are several Boston locations you must visit. The Bow and Arrow Bar, Woodies L Street Tavern and of course Bunker Hill Community College in the Charlestown Neighborhood are local places actually used in the filming of the movie.

DO IT IF: You are a fan of the movie and want to see the local places transformed to the big screen.

SKIP IT IF: You have no will for hunting these sights.

LOCAL ADVICE: The Bow and Arrow Pub, which was located at the corner of Bow Street and Massachusetts Avenue in Cambridge, doubled as the Harvard bar in which Will met Skylar for the first time. The Dunkin' Donuts featured in the "How do you like them apples?" scene was next door to the pub at the time of the film's release.

I DID IT: ☐   www.imdb.com/title/tt0119217

DID YOU KNOW?

Filming took place between April and June 1997. Although the story is set in Boston, and many of the scenes were shot on location in the Greater Boston area, many of the interior shots were filmed at locations in Toronto, with the University of Toronto standing in for MIT and Harvard University.

42

STROLL THE BOSTON NAVY YARD

WHAT'S THE DEAL?   Originally opened in1801, the Boston Navy Yard is home to the U.S.S Constitution as well as the WWII era destroyer U.S.S Cassin Young. After the base's closing in 1974, 30 acres became the Boston National Historic Park.

DO IT IF: You are walking the freedom trail, it adjacent to the U.S.S. Constitution.

SKIP IT IF: You have had your fill of historical sights.

LOCAL ADVICE: If you like being transported back in time, the Boston Navy Yard is a place for you too see. The brick buildings are intact from the early 1800's and the courtyard still maintain the original granite pavers which lined the courtyard.

I DID IT: www.nps.gov/bost/learn/historyculture/cny.htm

DID YOU KNOW?

The Charlestown Navy Yard built, repaired, modernized, and resupplied ships for 174 years. From here ships and the sailors serving aboard set off to places around the globe. The ships that left this yard represented the United States on every continent and defended the nation through both times of war and peace.

43

TAKE THE FERRY TO P-TOWN

WHAT'S THE DEAL? Looking for an interesting day trip from Boston? From Mid-May through Mid-October, you can travel to Provincetown on Cape Cod in about 90 minutes, avoiding the long drive through summertime traffic. You can also bring a bike, but book ahead; this attraction can be sold out in the peak of the season.

DO IT IF: You have a day to spend outside of Boston.

SKIP IT IF: You do not have a full day to spare.

LOCAL ADVICE: If you want to escape the city and stroll the narrow streets of P- Town, the ferry trip is a good option. The drive from Boston to P-Town can be 3+ hours especially at the height of the summer season. This ferry is passenger only, so no cars or motorized vehicles allowed. You can take your pet or a bike for a fee, so reserve ahead and head to the Cape!

I DID IT: ☐ baystatecruisecompany.com

DID YOU KNOW?

If you do take the ferry trip to Provincetown, it's a very walkable downtown. The main street is Commercial Avenue which offers dozens of restaurant, coffee shops and local artisan galleries. There are some great local galleries offering amazing hand painted landscapes to take home with you as a reminder of your day trip.

44

RELAX AT A WATERFRONT PARK

WHAT'S THE DEAL? Boston's redevelopments especially in the south end and along the area of the big dig have created some great spaces where you can enjoy some waterfront views. A personal favorite is Christopher Columbus Park which is within a short walk to Long Wharf, Faneuil Hall and the North End.

DO IT IF: Sometimes you just need a rest!

SKIP IT IF: You are always on the go!!!

LOCAL ADVICE: A personal favorite is Christopher Columbus Park, just north of the Boston Long Wharf Marriott Hotel. There are benches if you wish to take a rest and the waterfront location offers plenty of great views of the active harbor just steps away. There is even a small playground if the little ones need something to keep them occupied.

I DID IT: ☐ www.cityofboston.gov/Parks

DID YOU KNOW?

For such a thickly settled urban area, Boston also offers a wide variety of green spaces as well. There are more than 2,000 acres of neighborhood parks, playgrounds, tot lots, and athletic facilities in the City of Boston.

45

SOLVE A FAMOUS ROBBERY

WHAT'S THE DEAL? The Isabella Steward Gardner museum houses one of the world's most valuable private art collections. Isabella Gardner, the wife of a wealthy shipping magnate, constructed the museum in 1903 to hold her private collection. On the morning of March 18th, 1990 while most of Boston was winding down St. Patrick's Day celebrations, 2 men dressed as police officers entered the museum. 13 works of art were stolen and never recovered, with a reported value of $500 million dollars.

DO IT IF: You fancy yourself as an amateur art sleuth.

SKIP IT IF: You know what's good for ya.

LOCAL ADVICE: Isabella Stewart Gardner collected and carefully displayed a collection comprised of more than 7500 paintings, sculptures, furniture, textiles, silver, ceramics, 1500 rare books, and 7000 archival objects-from ancient Rome, Medieval Europe, Renaissance Italy, Asia, the Islamic world. One of the hidden assets of the museum is the beautiful landscapes and gardens as well. It is a go to spot for many locals to relax and unwind from the hectic lifestyle that sometimes accompanies life in Boston.

I DID ☐ www.gardnermuseum.o

DID YOU KNOW?

Despite some promising leads in the past, the Gardner theft remains unsolved. The Museum, the FBI, and the US Attorney's office are still seeking viable leads that could result in safe return of the art. It would be worth your time to solve this by the way,the museum is offering a 10 million dollar reward!

The Museum is offering a reward of $10 million for information leading directly to the recovery of all 13 works in good condition. A separate reward of $100,000 is being offered for the return of the Napoleonic eagle finial.

46

AVOID ALBERT DESALVO

WHAT'S THE DEAL? Terror swept the streets of Boston in 1964 with the deaths of 13 women between the ages of 19 and 85. Most of the women were sexually assaulted, then strangled with a piece of their own clothing. The "Boston Strangler" was finally arrested and sentenced to life in prison. In prison, Desalvo recanted his confession that he was the strangler, but before he could be re-tried, he was murdered by another inmate.

DO IT IF: You are a fan of unsolved murders or serial killers.

SKIP IT IF: It might cause you nightmares.

LOCAL ADVICE: There is still speculation to this day that Desalvo was responsible for all of the killings. DNA evidence did link him to 1 murder, the evidence is inconclusive for the others linked to "The Boston Strangler."

I DID IT: www.biography.com/crime-figure/albert-de-salvo

DID YOU KNOW?

DeSalvo was the subject of the 1968 film The Boston Strangler, starring Tony Curtis as DeSalvo, and Henry Fonda and George Kennedy as the homicide detectives who apprehend him. It assumed that DeSalvo was guilty, and it portrayed him as suffering from multiple personality disorder DeSalvo was never diagnosed with, nor even suspected of, having that disorder.

47

WATCH A WHALE

WHAT'S THE DEAL?   From the Long Wharf area of Boston, you will find seasonal whale watching trips to a national marine wildlife sanctuary. Frequently spotted on these 3-to-4-hour excursions are humpbacks, finbacks and even white sided dolphins.

DO IT IF: You desire to see the magnificent mammals in their natural habitat.

SKIP IT IF: 3 to 4 hours at sea might make you woozy.

LOCAL ADVICE: The Whale watches take you Stellwagen Bank Marine Sanctuary, a rich feeding ground for whales, dolphins, sea birds and other marine creatures. You will learn about them from New England Aquarium naturalists who are always on board to share their extensive knowledge. This a great activity to share with the family or a fun group outing that everyone will remember for years to come.

I DID IT: ☐   www.bostonharborcruises.com/whale-watch

DID YOU KNOW?

Stellwagen Bank National Marine Sanctuary, a wild ocean place near an urban world, sits east of Boston, Massachusetts between Cape Ann and Cape Cod. Historically important as a fishing ground, New England's only national marine sanctuary now reigns as a premier whale watching destination.

48

ROLL THE DICE

WHAT'S THE DEAL? The sparkling new Boston encore offers the glamor of Las Vegas style casinos without hopping a flight out of town.

DO IT IF: You want a night of Vegas style entertainment, without leaving town.

SKIP IT IF: It's Vegas or Bust for your gambling trip.

LOCAL ADVICE: The resort is in a commercial-industrial area on the Mystic River, about 5 miles from downtown Boston. Public amenities of the year-round harbor walk include a picnic park, paths for bikers and pedestrians, viewing decks, waterfront dining and retail, a performance lawn, floral displays, boat docks, and public art. The casino has been a local job creator and really improved a local eye sore with a glimmering new hotel and casino complex.

I DID IT: www.encorebostonharbor.com

DID YOU KNOW?

The development of the Wynn Encore rehabilitated a 33-acre parcel of land previously used for industrial purposes.It opened on June 23, 2019, at a total cost of $2.6 billion.

49

EAT AT A TEST KITCHEN

WHAT'S THE DEAL? If you are looking for a fresh and innovative take on traditional seafood, look no further than LTK. The iconic Boston seafood restaurant Legal Seafood tries new and fresh ideas in their test kitchen restaurant in the terminal at Logan Airport.

DO IT IF: You want to try new takes and dishes on fresh seafood.

SKIP IT IF: Your seafood must be served in a traditional way.

LOCAL ADVICE: LTK is located beyond security near the Delta Shuttle gates. They would love to have you dine with them but understand if you have to grab-and-go with their pre-wrapped sandwiches or other take-out items. In the case of layovers or delays, our restaurant and bar are a perfect port to pass the time. And yes, they do offer traditional seafood just in case. Logan airport offers some great people watching as well.

I DID IT: legalseafoods.com/restaurants/boston-legal-test-kitchen -logan-airport-terminal-a-42

DID YOU KNOW?

The brand Legal Sea Foods was born in 1950 with the Berkowitz family opening of a fish market in the Inman Square neighborhood of Cambridge, Massachusetts. At that time there was also a related family business adjacent to the market, a grocery store, known as Legal Cash Market, where customers were given "Legal Stamps" with their purchases.

50

FIND THE PURPLE GLASS

WHAT'S THE DEAL? On Boston's tony Beacon Hill, it is kind of a local status symbol if you own a colonial brownstone with purple panes of glass. It signifies original hand-blown windows from the 1800's.

DO IT IF: You appreciate artisans and the enduring work they created that lasts to this day.

SKIP IT IF: You sweat the small stuff.

LOCAL ADVICE: Another of Boston's historic neighborhoods, Beacon Hill is one of the most affluent. The hand-blown glass with a hint of purple is a way for the ultra-wealthy to subtly display their wealth. The locals refer to them as Lavenders and the purple color denotes a certain status of Boston royalty. Keep an eye open for local resident and former Senator John Kerry.

I DID IT: ☐ www.beaconhillonline.com

DID YOU KNOW?

Many of Beacon Hill's famed purple windows were the result of a nineteenth-century mistake. Between 1818 and 1824, an English company sent shipments of glass that contained too much manganese oxide and turned a purple hue when exposed to sunlight.

When the windows were installed in a number of townhouses in Beacon Hill, the glass appeared normal, but after being exposed to sunlight for an extended period of time, it began to turn purple. One local expert discovered sunlight to be the culprit.

51

EXPERIENCE THE PEABODY ESSEX MUSEUM

WHAT'S THE DEAL? The Peabody Essex, located a short train ride north of Boston, is one of our nation's most venerable and vibrant art museums. This innovative gallery offers many different art forms from the 1700's to present day. They include photography, painting and even sculpture presented in a fresh and unique manner. It is not just art placed on a wall; it's a celebration of people's creativity.

DO IT IF: You want to see almost every kind of art form and collectable in 1 place.

SKIP IT IF: Salem is too fahr.

LOCAL ADVICE: The trip to PEM is like visiting a museum of potpourri. From witch trial exhibits, to maritime art, ship's figurehead, modern photography and even entire houses, they really do have it all. One of the most intriguing exhibits is Yin Yu Tang, an 18th-century Chinese merchant's house transported from China and reassembled here at the museum.

I DID IT: ☐ www.pem.org

DID YOU KNOW?

Founded in 1799, The Peabody Essex Museum has the distinction of being the oldest continuously operating and collecting museum in the United States. Far from a typical museum, it is more an amalgamation of entities, a collection of collections.

52

TAKE A FLIGHT

WHAT'S THE DEAL? Boston's Airport, Logan International, literally offers connections around the globe. You can fly as close as Nantucket or as far as London, Istanbul, Panama City or even Beijing, non-stop.

DO IT IF: You are a jet setter.

SKIP IT IF: You never leave "southie." Yah, everything I need is right here.

LOCAL ADVICE: Located on an island in Boston harbor, Boston is blessed to have a connection to basically any place in the world and the Airport is the gateway to New England. The biggest drawback can be the weather, which can cause delays or bumpy landings.

I DID IT: ☐   www.massport.com/logan-airport

DID YOU KNOW?

General Edward Lawrence Logan Airport is an international airport that is located mostly in East Boston. It opened in 1923, covers 2,384 acres , has six runways and four passenger terminals, and employs an estimated 16,000 people. In fact, you can reach 56 international destinations via nonstop flights out of the Boston airport, according to Massport.

53

MARVEL AT THE "BIG DIG"

WHAT'S THE DEAL? The massive highway project finally completed in 2002, with a cost of over 20 billion dollars, was a modern marvel of engineering. Construction crews buried the main expressway under the crowded Boston streets freeing up greenspaces and eliminating the old elevated central artery highway.

DO IT IF: You marvel at modern engineering feats.

SKIP IT IF: Massive cost over runs annoy you.

LOCAL ADVICE: The Central Artery/ Tunnel project locally became known as the Big Dig. This project was developed in response to traffic congestion on Boston's historically tangled streets which were laid out centuries before the advent of the automobile. Although plagued with billions of dollars of cost over runs, fraud and taking more than 15 years to complete, it was well worth the effort. Besides creating thousands of jobs, it put the traffic beneath the city and open beautiful green spaces.

I DID IT: ☐ www.mass.gov/info-details/the-big-dig-project-background

DID YOU KNOW?

The Big Dig was the most expensive highway project in US history. The project was originally scheduled to be completed in 1998 at an estimated cost of $2.8 billion However, the project was completed in December 2007 at a cost of over $8.08 billion

54

THROW LOBSTER AT YOUR   ENEMY

WHAT'S THE DEAL? Believe it or not, when settlers first arrived in Boston, there were so many lobsters in the harbor; they literally crawled onto the streets. The superstitious Puritans thought they were a curse from god and would use the crustations to hurl toward someone they disliked, Similar to giving the finger in today's polite society.

DO IT IF: You have an enemy you wish to enrage.

SKIP IT IF: You prefer dueling.

LOCAL ADVICE: It is hard to imagine who the first person was who actually cooked and ate a lobster, but obviously someone did. It is currently one of Boston's most requested menu item and almost every local restaurant offers this crustacean as a dining option.

I DID IT: ☐   www.timeout.com/boston/restaurants/
best-lobster-in-boston

DID YOU KNOW?

Beantown chefs have evolved and realized Lobster is way to valuable to throw around. They have come up with numerous creative ways to consume this delicacy like Lobster rolls, Lobster mac and cheese, Lobster pizza and even lobster and waffles.

55

CALL 98.5

WHAT'S THE DEAL? As you have probably realized, Bostonians are passionate about their local sports teams. And New Englanders are known to be great 2nd guessers and Monday Morning quarterbacks. What's the solution? Air your sports grievances on local sports talk radio.

DO IT IF: You need to re hash the game for 4 hours after literally just watching the game.

SKIP IT IF: You can't stand to hear grown adults whine about a child's game...for hours on end!

LOCAL ADVICE: Boston sports fan have gravitated to the wildly popular 98.5 the sports hub as an around the clock sports fans dream. Throughout the day various hosts delve into a variety of sports takes and callers spend the day 2nd guessing the coach's failings, player miscues and executives lack of moves around the trading deadline.

I DID IT: ☐   985thesportshub.com

DID YOU KNOW?

Felger & Mazz is a Marconi Award-winning afternoon radio show on 98.5.The show first aired on August 13, 2009 with the launch of WBZ-FM's sports talk radio station. The show is known for its negative demeanor towards local sports teams, hot takes, and willingness to go after local teams and players.

56

TAKE A CLASS

WHAT'S THE DEAL? The greater Boston area is home to some of the finest colleges and universities in the world. Boston College, Boston University, Northeastern, Harvard, MIT and even Emerson College of the performing arts make this area the epicenter for higher education worldwide.

DO IT IF: You wish to expand your mental horizons.

SKIP IT IF: Been there, done that.

LOCAL ADVICE: Boston prides itself as a haven for higher education. Students from literally all over the globe flock to the area for a life changing education. A word of advice if you are planning to visit Boston in early September, it will be busy with returning college students and their families.

I DID IT:

DID YOU KNOW?

Boston University is considered the largest of the Boston area schools with enrollment of more than 30,000 students. Harvard University is the oldest founded in 1636.

57

DINE AT THE OLDEST RESTAURANT IN THE U.S.A.

WHAT'S THE DEAL? The Union Oyster house has been serving hungry Bostonians since 1826. Housed in a pre-revolutionary war building, this eatery was a favorite of Massachusetts lawyer and statesman Daniel Webster. It also has the distinction of being the first restaurant to hand out toothpicks to its patrons.

DO IT IF: You enjoy dining in historic locations.

SKIP IT IF: You need the trappings of modern dining rooms.

LOCAL ADVICE: Originally operating at Atwood and Bacon oyster bar, the Union Oyster house has stood the test of time at 41 Union Street. Of course, oysters are their claim to fame, they also offer a great bowl of baked beans.

I DID IT: ☐ Unionoysterhouse.com

DID YOU KNOW?

The Union Oyster House has had a number of famous people in history as diners, including the Kennedy family and Daniel Webster. Webster was known for regularly consuming at least six plates of oysters. In 1796 Louis Philippe, king of France from 1830 to 1848, lived in exile on the second floor.

ENTER THE GOLDEN DOME

WHAT'S THE DEAL? Completed in 1798, on land owned by the first governor of Massachusetts John Hancock, the State House was designed by architect Charles Bulfinch. The original dome was plated in copper by Paul Revere in 1802, then gold leaf in 1874. In a 1997 renovation the dome was re-gilded in 23 carat gold leaf at a cost of roughly $300,000. Tours of the state house are weekdays 10 am to 3:30 pm and are free of charge.

DO IT IF: Touring state capitals is on your personal bucket list.

SKIP IT IF: State Capitals are small potatoes.

LOCAL ADVICE: If you do not wish to attend an organized tour, self-guided materials are also available. Look for the fish in the house chamber. The Sacred Cod, a five-foot wooden codfish and a symbol of the importance of the fishing industry to the State of Massachusetts's economy.

I DID IT: ☐ www.sec.state.ma.us/trs/trsidx.htm

DID YOU KNOW?

In addition to the Massachusetts State House, Architect Charles Bulfinch also designed the original State House in

Hartford, Connecticut and the State Capitol in Augusta,

Maine.

59

VISIT A COLONIAL PRINTING PRESS

WHAT'S THE DEAL? An actual colonial era printing operation still exists in Boston, the printing office of Edes and Gill. Located in the historic Clough house on the freedom trail, this living history museum lets you experience first-hand how the Boston Gazette was printed.

DO IT IF: The history of the printed word fascinates you.

SKIP IT IF: You thought the printing press? That's so 1750's..

LOCAL ADVICE: The Edes and Gill print shop offers visitors a unique personal encounter with history and colonial printing. As Boston's only colonial trade experience and only colonial living history interpretive experience, their historic equipment, live demonstrations, interpreters and historic settings enable new levels of understanding how colonial printing affected communities and sparked a revolution in America.

I DID IT: ☐ Bostongazette.org

DID YOU KNOW?

On April 7, 1755, Edes and Gill became the proprietors of The Boston Gazette and Country Journal. According to historians the Boston Gazette, was arguably the most influential newspaper the country has ever known, got us into the Revolutionary War, sped up the course of the war and may have even determined the outcome of the war.

RIDE A CAROUSEL

WHAT'S THE DEAL? Opening in 2013 in its location next to the Frog Pond, the Carousel is an American masterpiece built by the Chance Morgan Ride Company of Wichita, Kansas. The Carousel features a variety of Bradley and Kaye horses, unique wildlife figures, and a chariot. It is open seasonally mid-April thru October.

DO IT IF: You want to rekindle a carefree time in your life or spend some quality time with the kids.

SKIP IT IF: You not into riding in circles.

LOCAL ADVICE: With its oak floor, beveled glass mirrors, and a standard pie top with a lighted crown, these features give the Carousel a classic style. It is especially beautiful when all lit up in the evening. If it is available try to ride the zebra!

I DID IT: ☐ Bostonfrogpond.com

DID YOU KNOW?

The Allan Herschell Company, the most prolific maker of carousels, specialized in producing portable machines which could be used by traveling carnival operators. The Company produced over 3,000 hand carved wooden carousels and out-produced all of its rivals in the carousel industry.

61

STROLL ACORN STREET

WHAT'S THE DEAL? Just off of Louisburg Square, in the upscale Beacon Hill neighborhood, you will find perhaps the most photographed lane in town: Acorn Street. One of the last true cobblestone streets in the city, it harkens back to the colonial period when many of Boston's thoroughfares were paved in this manner.

DO IT IF: Historic lanes are nostalgic and picturesque to you.

SKIP IT IF: Your tired of strolling the historic streets of Boston.

LOCAL ADVICE: Acorn Street is currently a private way owned and governed by a neighborhood association. Neighbors retained ownership and control of this private way to prevent the City of Boston from paving it in in the 1980's. It is an affluent neighborhood and visitors are asked to move quietly and quickly through this area. One neat thing is if you go in the summer you will see weeds and grass growing up through the century's old cobblestones.

I DID IT: ☐ acornstreetassociation.com

DID YOU KNOW?

In the years before the Civil War, this area of Beacon Hill was part of a large African American community. the largest in Boston at the time. Further up Beacon Hill were homes of wealthy white families. Many free Blacks who lived along Acorn Street and nearby worked in those homes.

62

LISTEN TO THE POPS

WHAT'S THE DEAL? The Boston Symphony Orchestra gave its inaugural concert in 1881, realizing the dream of its founder, the Civil War veteran and philanthropist Henry Lee Higginson, who dreamed of a great and permanent orchestra in his hometown of Boston. Today the orchestra or pops as it is locally known, reaches millions of listeners, not only through its concert performances in Boston and at Tanglewood, but also via the internet, radio, television, and tours.

DO IT IF: You live for a big symphony orchestra.

SKIP IT IF: A guitar and harmonica are enough instruments for your ears.

LOCAL ADVICE: Boston Pops primarily consists of musicians from the BSO, although generally not all the first-chair players. The orchestra performs a spring season of popular music and a holiday program in December. For the Pops, the seating on the floor of Symphony Hall is reconfigured from auditorium seating to banquet/cafe seating. Identified with its long-time director Arthur Fiedler, the orchestra has recorded extensively, made frequent tours, and appeared regularly on television.

I DID IT: ☐ www.bso.org

DID YOU KNOW?

When Boston Symphony Orchestra musicians are not on stage at Symphony Hall, half of them are across the street at The New England Conservatory, teaching the next generation of orchestra players.

63

LEARN ABOUT THE LIBRARY

WHAT'S THE DEAL? Established in 1848, the Boston Public Library (BPL) was the first large free municipal library in the United States. The Boston Public Library's first building of its own was a former schoolhouse located on Mason Street but with over 16,000 books this location was too small. In 1986, the library expanded to the McKim Building on Copely Square where you'll find fine collections of rare books and manuscripts, maps, and prints, and splendid gallery space for displaying the numerous treasures assembled over the past 160 years.

DO IT IF: You yearn to learn.

SKIP IT IF: You prefer audio books.

LOCAL ADVICE: Amenities include a restaurant and café, a peaceful inner courtyard, several comfortable and wifi accessible inviting reading areas. It almost feels like a neighborhood bookstore more than a public library.

I DID IT: ☐ www.bpl.org

DID YOU KNOW?

The first thing you will notice is the impressive building in which the library is housed. In 1887 the prestigious New York firm of McKim, Mead, and White was chosen for the projet and a Renaissance style design based on the Bibliotheque Ste-Geneviève in Paris was created here in Boston.

64

SAMPLE COLONIAL CHOCOLATE

WHAT'S THE DEAL? Taste the sweetest side of the American Revolution! When walking into this shop, located inside the Old North Church, you will be able to touch, taste, smell, and experience 18th-century chocolate as it was enjoyed by some of Boston's most famous Revolutionary-era citizens. You will discover where chocolate comes from and how it is made. You even get a free taste of the delicious drink enjoyed by John and Abigail Adams.

DO IT IF: You crave colonial chocolate.

SKIP IT IF: Your candy must be imported from Europe.

LOCAL ADVICE: The chocolate program offers an interactive education experience about the triangle trade, how it supported the economy of colonial Boston and its growth into the city we know today. The program is located in the historic Clough House on the Old North Church & Historic Site campus. Admittance into the historic chocolate program is included with your admission.

I DID IT: ☐ www.oldnorth.com/explore/historic-chocolate-program

DID YOU KNOW?

It's thought the first American chocolate house opened in Boston in 1682. By 1773, cocoa beans were a major American colony import and chocolate was enjoyed by people of all classes.

65

M.O.B.A

WHAT'S THE DEAL? One the most creative museums in all of Boston, the Museum of Bad Art, is truly a must see. M.O.B.A actually has 2 locations to house the ever growing collection of truly hideous, yet humorous exhibits. The collections are located in the basement of the Somerville Theatre, next to the men's room and the lobby of Brookline Public Access Television.

DO IT IF: Art is in the eye of the beholder.

SKIP IT IF: You are only into the works of the European Masters.

LOCAL ADVICE: Partially humorous, partially comical and partially sad that someone would actually spend time creating some of these works of art. The museum is really in the basement of the Somerville Theatre, so go see a movie and browse some bad art! They also display their entire collection online...It is well worth a look.

I DID IT: museumofbadart.org

DID YOU KNOW?

The Museum of Bad Art is a privately owned museum whose stated aim is "to celebrate the labor of artists whose work would be displayed and appreciated in no other forum. Its permanent collection includes over 700 pieces of "art too bad to be ignored", 25 to 35 of which are on public display at any one time.

66

STOP AND SMELL THE ROSES

WHAT'S THE DEAL? Once a dirty backwater swamp, landscape architect Frederick Law Olmstead transformed this are known as the Back Bay fens into part of a greenspace known as the emerald necklace. In 1910, the damming of the Charles River turned the Fens into a freshwater marsh. Over time, new features such as ball fields and the Kelleher Rose Garden employing the more formal landscape style popular in the 1920s were added.

DO IT IF: Historic gardens and beautiful flowers entice you.

SKIP IT IF: You're allergic to nature.

LOCAL ADVICE: Surrounded by some of Boston's leading educational, cultural and medical institutions, the Back Bay Fens is an eclectic mix of formal and community gardens, ball fields, memorials and historic structures. With places for passive recreation and active pursuits, the park offers a range of experiences such as gardening and sports and is a popular spot for birders.

I DID IT: ☐ www.emeraldnecklace.org/park-overview/back-bay-fens

DID YOU KNOW?

Inside the Fens,you will also find the oldest remaining wartime "Victory Garden" planted by citizens in 1941 during World War II to provide much needed fruits and vegetables. Today it is a well-loved community garden.

67

CONQUER HEARTBREAK HILL

WHAT'S THE DEAL? This would definitely be one of the more physically challenging items on the Boston Bucket List. Heartbreak Hill is a section of the Boston Marathon which has claimed many a victim over the race's storied history. Normally not a steep incline to most runners, the final hill of the marathon comes just after the 20-mile mark. But after clearing the top, downtown Boston and the finish line aren't too far off.

DO IT IF: You want a physical and mental challenge.

SKIP IT IF: 26 miles feels like a marathon.

LOCAL ADVICE: The Boston Marathon does allow a few thousand people who are affiliated with one of the marathon's official charities run in the marathon without having to qualify. However, everyone else must qualify by completing a certified marathon in the required time based on their age.

I DID IT: ☐ www.baa.org

DID YOU KNOW?

Traditionally held on Patriots' Day, the third Monday of April. Begun in 1897, the event was inspired by the success of the first marathon competition in the 1896 Summer Olympics. The Boston Marathon is the world's oldest annual marathon and ranks as one of the world's best-known road racing events.

STROLL THE ESPLANADE

WHAT'S THE DEAL?   Once the muddy riverbank of the Charles, the esplanade stretches along Storrow Drive, featuring some of Boston's most beautiful green space. Created when the Charles River dam was completed in 1910, the parks feature ballfields, picnic pavilions, boating facilities and the world famous band shell.

DO IT IF: You enjoy scenic walks along a river with great views of the Boston Skyline.

SKIP IT IF: Scenic walks in urban riverfront parks just aren't for you.

LOCAL ADVICE: The Esplanade is one of Boston's best loved parks with stunning views of the Charles River. From the filling of the Back Bay to the beginning of Storrow Drive, the Esplanade was built in stages fulfilling the vision of landscape architect Charles Eliot. Today, the onetime muddy bogs are now busy with walkers, joggers, skaters, and bikers.

I DID IT: ☐   www.esplanadeassociation.org

DID YOU KNOW?

Charles Eliot is best remembered for pioneering principles of regional planning, naturalistic systems approach to landscape architecture, and laying the groundwork for conservancies across the world. He was a once an apprentice to the pioneer of landscape architecture, Fredrick Law Olmstead.

WATCH "THE GAME"

WHAT'S THE DEAL? The intense rivalry dating back to 1875, matches the Ivy League institutions of Harvard and Yale in traditionally the final game of their football season. Typically, the season record isn't very important to the fiercely enthusiastic alums attending, just beat the hated rival and the year is judged a success.

DO IT IF: You live for the Crim-son!

SKIP IT IF: You find football barbaric or it's Ivy League Football.

LOCAL ADVICE: As the second-oldest rivalry in college football, the Harvard-Yale game is more than just a football game. It's The Game. For many alumni, it's also a chance to reconnect and reaffirm friendships forged decades ago. Whether joining in person or attending one of the many viewing parties, alumni from across the globe come together each year to celebrate The Game and cheer on Harvard.

I DID IT: ☐ alumni.harvard.edu/harvard-yale

DID YOU KNOW?

T.A.D Jones, a former Yale coach told once tried to motivate his team by telling them"Gentlemen, you are now going out to play football against Harvard. Never again in your whole life will you do anything so important."

70

PAY TRIBUTE TO ROBERT GOULD SHAW

WHAT'S THE DEAL? You may not know the name, but if you have ever seen the movie Glory, you are familiar with Colonel Shaw's actions. Born into a Boston abolitionist family, Colonel Shaw led the 54th Massachusetts infantry, an all-black regiment, in an attack on a confederate fort. Fort Wagner, just outside of Charleston, South Carolina was heavily defended and Colonel Shaw and many of his men were killed in the raid. He is forever immortalized leading his men, in a statue just across the street from the Massachusetts state capital.

DO IT IF: You admire people who stood up for what they believed in.

SKIP IT IF: You are spending your time in the North End.

LOCAL ADVICE: If you are at the State Capital or even Boston Common, take a quick look at the impressive monument. The large sculptural memorial by Augustus Saint-Gaudens has the likeness of Shaw on horseback, accompanied by members of the 54th Regiment, as they marched through Boston to depart for the war.

I DID IT: ☐ www.nps.gov/boaf/learn/historyculture/shaw.htm

DID YOU KNOW?

Shaw's friends and family believed it was an honor for him to be buried with his soldiers. His father publicly proclaimed that he was proud to know that his son had been buried with his troops, befitting his role as a soldier and a crusader for emancipation.

71

HOIST A HARPOON

WHAT'S THE DEAL? Three college friends with a love for beer started a craft brewery on the side of Boston Harbor in 1986. Today they produce over a dozen varieties of local favorites and the brewery offers a tasting room, tours of the facility as well as a European style beer hall with some of the best views of the city skyline.

DO IT IF: You enjoy a local seasonal craft beer served at the source.

SKIP IT IF: You are kind of beered out.

LOCAL ADVICE: So if you enjoyed Mike's pastry in the North End, we may have found the beer for you. An even more decadent take on our Cannoli Stout collaboration with the famous Mike's Pastry of Boston's North End. Brewed using Mike's hand-made cannoli shells, cocoa nibs, lactose, and vanilla to re-create the flavor profile of their famed dessert, this higher-strength rendition was aged for two months in premium rye whiskey barrels for added layers of vanilla, spice, and caramel. Nothing like a beer for your sweet tooth!

I DID IT: ☐ Harpoonbrewery.com

DID YOU KNOW?

One neat thing about Harpoon is it employee owned. They want to see their products succeed and their customers have positive experiences when they try the beer or enjoy a pretzel in the Harpoon Beer Hall. It is a great incentive in helping Harpoon Brewery stay independent and remaining dedicated to their mission: brewing great beer and sharing unforgettable beer drinking experiences.

72

FIND THE GRAVE OF MARY DYER

WHAT'S THE DEAL? One of the earliest believers in the Quaker movement in the colonies, Mary Dyer certainly was willing to sacrifice it all for her beliefs. She repeatedly traveled from Rhode Island to puritan Boston to profess her views and was repeatedly exiled and threatened with hanging. Finally on June 1, 1660, the execution was carried out and Mary Dyer became a symbol of martyrdom and freedom of religion. She was buried in an unmarked grave somewhere in Boston Common.

DO IT IF: You want to remember an early advocate of religious freedom.

SKIP IT IF: You are strict Puritan who thinks she was wrong.

LOCAL ADVICE: Mary Dyer had a good life in Newport, Rhode Island. Along with her husband, one of the 9 founders of the city, Mary had a large farm just north of downtown. But she was staunch in her beliefs eventually sacrificing her life for what she believed in. Since her grave was unmarked, a statue was placed in front of the State House to honor her memory and sacrifice.

I DID IT: ☐ bwht.org/beacon-hill

DID YOU KNOW?

Mary Dyer was an English and colonial American Puritan turned Quaker who was hanged in Boston, Massachusetts Bay Colony, for repeatedly defying a Puritan law banning Quakers from the colony. She is one of the four executed Quakers known as the Boston martyrs.

73

GO NORTH TO SEE WITCHES

WHAT'S THE DEAL? Just a short trip north of Boston, you will discover the seaside village of Salem, famous for its witch trials of the late 17th century. Hear the stories of why 20 people were put to death in the witchcraft hysteria.

DO IT IF: You wish to see witch city for yourself.

SKIP IT IF: You are superstitious that someone will put a spell on you.

LOCAL ADVICE: Salem is a great town to visit just up the road from downtown Boston, 11 months of the year. There is a colonial city center, numerous witch related attractions and the house of the 7 gables. But unless you enjoy massive Halloween crowds, avoid October visits all costs. Parking in the city is difficult even at non- Halloween weekends. During Halloween festivities, you will need to park miles from downtown and be shuttled in and out to the revelries.

I DID IT: ☐ salemwitchmuseum.com

DID YOU KNOW?

Over the course of the year 1692, approximately 150 people across Essex County were jailed for witchcraft. Ultimately, nineteen people were hanged and one man was pressed to death after being examined by the Court of Oyer and Terminer. This was the largest witch-hunt to ever take place in America, and would be the last large-scale panic to take place in the New World.

74

VISIT THE PATRIOTS HALL OF FAME

WHAT'S THE DEAL? Just a short ride south of Boston, you will find the New England Patriots Hall of Fame at Gillette Stadium. Even if you aren't a Patriots fan, the museum and hall house artifacts, game balls and memorabilia from the early days of the AFL and NFL, right up the modern game loved by millions of fans.

DO IT IF: You are a big Patriots fan or even just the N.F.L.

SKIP IT IF: You are still mad at Bill Belichick for Spy Gate.

LOCAL ADVICE: Growing up in New England, the Patriots were historically near the bottom of the bottom of the standings. Will Robert Kraft buying the team, the hiring of Bill Belichick and the drafting of Tom Brady in the 6th round, the franchise's fortunes have improved. Never in my wildest dreams would I expect this team to win 6 super bowls over 20 years. So head to Gillette Stadium, buy some memorabilia at the pro shop and see the Hall of Fame.

I DID IT: ☐ www.thehallatpatriotplace.com

DID YOU KNOW?

The Hall has two floors of exhibit galleries full of interesting artifacts, touch screens and interactive entertainment. Guests can walk back through team history by viewing traditional artifact cases or through a digital timeline featuring awesome photos, videos, newspaper clippings, rosters, results and more.

75

HIT THE BEACH

WHAT'S THE DEAL? Just south of downtown in nearby Dorchester, you will find Malibu and Savin Hill Beaches. A new playground, new sand, new lighting and additional landscaping add to the atmosphere at these beaches. Malibu Beach has a protected swimming area and a bathhouse. Savin Hill Beach has a kid's lot, baseball fields and a protected swimming area as well. Don't forget your swimsuit!

DO IT IF: You want to hit the beach, but do not want to travel to fahr.

SKIP IT IF: You are visiting in January.

LOCAL ADVICE: These are both popular local beaches especially on hot summer days. Parking is limited so there is an option to ride the red line to get you to the south side shore line. And remember no dogs allowed during the summer.

I DID IT: ☐ www.mass.gov/locations/savin-hill-and-malibu-beach

DID YOU KNOW?

Savin Hill and Malibu Beach is the perfect place to go for a beach day without having to leave the city. This awsome beach allows doggies during the off-season, and the surrounding park welcomes them year round. The beach looks out over the Dorchester Bay Basin, with views of the nearby Dorchester Yacht Club.

76

EXPLORE THE OTIS HOUSE

WHAT'S THE DEAL? Otis House is the last surviving federal style mansion in Bowdoin Square in Boston's West End neighborhood. Charles Bulfinch, designer of the Massachusetts state capital, designed the property for Harrison Gray Otis, a lawyer who was influential in developing nearby Beacon Hill, served in Congress, and was mayor of Boston.

DO IT IF: Charles Bulfinch's architectural works inspire you.

SKIP IT IF: You think bulfinch is for the birds.

LOCAL ADVICE: Take a tour of Otis House to learn about the family's life in the Federal era and the later history of the house, when it served as a clinic and a middle-class boarding house. The restoration of Otis House and its brilliantly colored wallpapers, carpeting, and high-style furnishings is based on meticulous historical and scientific research. Otis House is a National Historic Landmark, and the home of the Historic New England Library and Archives.

I DID IT: ☐ www.historicnewengland.org/ historic- properties/homes/otis-house

DID YOU KNOW?

Charles Bulfinch was an early American architect, and has been regarded by many as the first native-born American to practice architecture as a profession. Bulfinch split his career between his native Boston, Massachusetts, and Washington, D.C., where he served as Commissioner of Public Building and built the United States Capitol rotunda and dome.

77

DISCOVER A FREE CHURCH

WHAT'S THE DEAL?   Thomas Paul, an African-American preacher from New Hampshire, led worship meetings at Faneuil Hall. Paul, with twenty of his members, officially formed the First African Baptist Church in 1805.The African Meeting House, as it came to be commonly called, was completed the next year. At the public dedication on December 6, 1806, the first-floor pews were reserved for all those "benevolently disposed to the Africans," while the black members sat in the balcony of their new meeting house.

DO IT IF: You want to see symbols of religious freedom.

SKIP IT IF: No church for you.

LOCAL ADVICE: In addition to serving as a spiritual center for the community, the African Meeting House was the chief cultural, educational, and political nexus of Boston's black community. The African School held classes in a room on the first floor of the meeting house from 1808 until 1835, when it moved into the new Abiel Smith School. Classes returned to the meeting house in 1849 when most African Americans chose to withdraw their children from the Smith School in order to protest against segregated education.

I DID IT: ☐   www.nps.gov/boaf/learn/historyculture/churches

DID YOU KNOW?

Abolitionists including William Lloyd Garrison, Maria Stewart, Wendell Phillips, Sarah Grimke, and Frederick Douglass all spoke at the meeting house. The Massachusetts General Colored Association, which was the first abolitionist organization in Boston, met at the African Meeting House, and in 1832 the New England Anti-Slavery Society was founded there.

78

EXPLORE THE ATHENAEUM

WHAT'S THE DEAL?   The Boston Athenæum is one of the oldest independent libraries in the United States. It was founded in 1807 by the Anthology Club of Boston, Massachusetts and is located at 10 1/2 Beacon Street on Beacon Hill. Just as a museum is a place for the muses who inspire art, so an athenæum is a place for Athena, the goddess of wisdom who inspires intellectual pursuits.

DO IT IF: You wish to expand your knowledge.

SKIP IT IF: You already know everything.

LOCAL ADVICE: Resources of the Boston Athenæum include a large circulating book collection; a public gallery; a rare books collection of over 100,000 volumes; an art collection of 100,000 paintings, sculptures, prints, drawings, photographs, and decorative arts; research collections including one of the world's most important collections of primary materials on the American Civil War; and a public forum offering lectures, readings, concerts, and other events.

I DID IT: www.bostonathenaeum.org

DID YOU KNOW?

The Athenæum supports a dynamic exhibition program and sponsors a lively variety of events such as lectures and concerts. It also serves as a stimulating center for discussions among scholars, bibliophiles, and a variety of community-interest groups.

79

CLIMB TO THE TOP OF THE CUSTOM HOUSE

WHAT'S THE DEAL? Originally built on the Boston Waterfront as the building that housed the collector of customs, this amazing structure is now an all-suite hotel. The clock tower added in 1915 by noted architects Peabody and Stearns, has one of the best views of the harbor and the nearby skyline, if you can find the entrance to the clock room.

DO IT IF: You enjoy a view from the top.

SKIP IT IF: You are terrified of heights and or small spaces.

LOCAL ADVICE: Not all bucket list items are easily achievable. To complete this item, you will probably need to be a guest at the custom house hotel, then be-friend someone from the maintenance staff who has a key to the clock room. But it is well worth the effort, the view from behind the clock is amazing.

I DID IT: ☐ www.marriott.com/hotels/travel/
bosch-marriotts-custom-house

DID YOU KNOW?

The Custom House Tower is a skyscraper in McKinley Square, in the Financial District neighborhood of Boston, Massachusetts. The original building was constructed in 1837–47 and was designed by Ammi Burnham Young in the Greek Revival style. The tower was designed by Peabody and Stearns and was added in 1913–15.

DISCOVER THE ZOO

WHAT'S THE DEAL? Perhaps the finest zoo on the East Coast, the Franklin Park zoo offers an unforgettable experience for all ages. The zoo is located in the northeast portion of Franklin Park, Boston's largest park and the last component of the city's famed Emerald Necklace.

DO IT IF: The zoo is for you!

SKIP IT IF: Wild animals out of their natural habitat is not your thing.

LOCAL ADVICE: The zoo was opened to the public in 1912 and managed by the City of Boston. Recently, the zoo has opened several new exhibits, including Bird's World, the Children's Zoo, and the African Tropical Forest. The zoo contains more than 220 species of wild and exotic animals.

I DID IT: www.zoonewengland.org

DID YOU KNOW?

Frederick Law Olmsted, the original landscape designer of Franklin Park, created plans for a future zoological garden. This plan, however, was to be a naturalistic area for native animals, rather than a traditional zoo. The Franklin Park Zoo officially opened to the public on October 4. 1912.

81

EXPERIENCE THE OPERA HOUSE

WHAT'S THE DEAL? The Boston Opera House is a performing arts venue located at 538 Washington St. in Boston Originally built as a movie palace, it opened on October 29, 1928 and was rededicated in 1980 as a home for the Opera Company of Boston. Completely restored in 2004, the theater currently serves as the home of the Boston Ballet and also presents touring Broadway shows. The building is an amazing venue to see live performances, bar none.

DO IT IF: You want to see a Broadway show right here in Beantown.

SKIP IT IF: Live is not your vibe.

LOCAL ADVICE: See the restoration that brought beauty and elegance back to this century-old theater. The Opera House is among the world's finest examples of vaudeville-era opulence and quality detailing. It is the only surviving work in Boston by distinguished American theater architect, Thomas Lamb. The 1-hour historical guided tour is a great way to see the restored the property if you can't make a live performance.

I DID IT: ☐ www.bostonoperahouseonline.com

DID YOU KNOW?

The opera house one of the finest examples of the vaudeville circuit palace at the pinnacle of its development. Designed in a combination of French and Italian styles by Thomas White Lamb, one of the foremost theatre architects of his day. Because it was constructed as a memorial to vaudeville's greatest impresario, it was built with a degree of luxury in its appointments that was almost unrivaled.

82

TAKE A PHOTO AT THE DUCK STATUE

WHAT'S THE DEAL? The city of Boston, the setting of the book, Make Way for the Ducklings, has embraced the story. In the Public Garden, where the Mallards eventually settled, a bronze statue has been erected of Mrs. Mallard and her eight ducklings. The statue, installed October 4, 1987, was a tribute to Author Robert McCloskey whose story has made the Boston Public Garden familiar to children throughout the world. Apparently the bronze statues never need polishing; they are kept shiny from all the children sitting on them.

DO IT IF: You liked the book Make way for Ducklings or statues of Ducks.

SKIP IT IF: You prefer geese, the Canadian kind perhaps?

LOCAL ADVICE: In addition to the ducks, you'll find lots more to see in the Public Garden: gorgeous flowers and trees, the famous Boston Swan Boats, impromptu concerts, and occasional weddings. Don't forget the annual Duckling Day Parade in May - the favorite Mother's Day event of many Boston moms.

I DID IT: ☐ www.boston-discovery-guide.com/ make-way-for-ducklings.html

DID YOU KNOW?

In Robert McCloskey's 1941 beloved children's classic, Make Way for Ducklings, Mr. and Mrs. Mallard come to Boston when searching for the perfect home for their soon-to-be family. They find the Public Garden, and decide to spend the night on the little island in the Lagoon.

FIND THE AREA'S BEST FRIED CLAMS

WHAT'S THE DEAL? According to the locals, there are 3 places in Boston to try, without having to go too far out of town. The consensus seems to be Royal Roast beef and Seafood in East Boston, Atlantic Fish Company in Back Bay and Neptune Oyster in the North End. Try them all and decide for yourself!

DO IT IF: You savor the chewy, salty fried mollusk fresh from the sea.

SKIP IT IF: Fried seafood is against your religion.

LOCAL ADVICE: Almost every Boston area restaurant has their take on the local favorite of fried clams. Remember for the true clam experience order whole belly Ipswich clams which are locally harvested and offer more flavor. Clam strips tend to be a bit dryer, are chewier and may not be locally sourced.

I DID IT: ☐   www.neptuneoyster.com
www.atlanticfish.com

DID YOU KNOW?

Fried clams are clam dipped in milk and then flour and deep-fried. Fried clams are an iconic food, "to New England, what barbecue is to the South". They tend to be served at seaside clam shacks. Clam rolls are fried clams served in a hot dog bun. Tartar sauce is the usual condiment.

84

BIKE BOSTON

WHAT'S THE DEAL? This activity might be for the braver souls among you, Boston traffic can be quite challenging. However, the city is adding numerous bike lanes and traffic sharing roads throughout downtown. There are also numerous" Hubways" which allow visitors to rent and return bicycles throughout the metro area.

DO IT IF: Biking in an urban environment excites you.

SKIP IT IF: You are a novice or used to riding bike only trails.

LOCAL ADVICE: The Arnold Arboretum might be the most scenic location to bike in greater Boston. This 125-year-old Boston city park and Harvard research center was designed by Frederick Law Olmsted and has a wonderful set of paved roads that are mostly closed to motorized traffic. Peters Hill, on which you now must walk the last 200 feet to the summit, provides the best natural view of Boston from within its boundaries.

I DID IT: ☐ www.visit-massachusetts.com/ boston/biking/

DID YOU KNOW?

Massachusetts has been deemed one of the most bike-friendly states in the country, with Boston and Cambridge considered the best places for cyclists in the Commonwealth in terms of biking commuter numbers, infrastructure and public safety.

85

SEE GHOSTS

WHAT'S THE DEAL? Boston is an old city by American standards, so one of the most common questions that arises is, is the city haunted? If the ask the folks conducting the Ghosts and Gravestones tour, the answer is a resounding yes. These brave souls will drive you to an early grave, while regaling some of Boston's most gruesome ghost stories. Join them if you dare!

DO IT IF: Finding Boston's haunted History is a must do for you.

SKIP IT IF: Haunted History gives you nightmares.

LOCAL ADVICE: The Ghosts and Gravestones tour gives a paranormal as well and dark history look at Boston after dark. We really enjoyed the special access you receive to the Granary Burying Ground, which is locked in the evening, except to tour attendees.

I DID IT: ☐ www.ghostsandgravestones.com/boston

DID YOU KNOW?

Boston's most infamous haunting is the lady in black, at Fort Warren on Georges Island just off the coast. The fort was used as a prison during the civil war for Confederate soldiers, and Mrs. Lanier traveled from Georgia to break out her husband. He was killed during the attempted escape and Mrs. Lanier was hanged and buried on the island. Her ghost dressed in black, still roams the island to this day!

GOLF THE FRANCIS OUIMET COURSE

WHAT'S THE DEAL? You may not recognize the name, but if you have seen the movie, The Greatest Game Ever Played, you are familiar with the story. It centers on a 20-year-old amateur golfer who ends up beating 2 heavily favored British players to win the 1913 U.S. Open golf Championship at the Brookline Country Club. Francis Ouimet is credited with popularizing golf in the United States, making it available to everyone, not just the very wealthy.

DO IT IF: You are friends with a member of the super exclusive Brookline Country Club.

SKIP IT IF: Mini golf is more your speed.

LOCAL ADVICE: The Country Club is not only the oldest country club in the United States, it is one of the largest in the Northeast. Nestled on 236 acres of land, just a few miles from Boston, TCC has approximately 1300 members. Our year-round club provides many facilities including 27 holes of golf, 5 indoor tennis courts, 4 outdoor tennis courts, paddle & squash courts, an Olympic-sized swimming pool with a cafe, curling, skeet shooting, skating & hockey and 5 guest rooms.

I DID IT: ☐   www.tcclub.org

DID YOU KNOW?

The Country Club holds an important place in golf history, as it is one of the five charter clubs that founded the United States Golf Association, and has hosted numerous USGA tournaments including the 1913,1963 ,1988 and 2022 U.S. Opens. The course also hosted contentious 1999 Ryder Cup.

87

FIND THE HOME OF BABE'S LAST TEAM

WHAT'S THE DEAL? Nickerson Stadium off of Commonwealth Avenue, on the Boston University campus, was the once the location of the National League's Boston Braves. In 1935 the fledgling baseball team traded for aging super star Babe Ruth to try to revive his career, and their box office, in the city where the Babe began his prodigious vocation. However, the plan went awry, the bambino retired by June 1st after hitting just .181 and the Braves finished in last place.

DO IT IF: You are a true Boston Baseball fan and yearn for the days when the Bambino was king.

SKIP IT IF: You thought Babe Ruth was a candy bar of some sort.

LOCAL ADVICE: He had joined the team thinking he would later be hired as a manager, but quickly came to realize that such an arrangement was not a possibility. Just days before Ruth finally quit, he had hit a home run so powerful it flew all the way out of Forbes Field -- the first home run to go that far. He played in his last game on May 30 and officially retired several days later.

I DID IT: ☐   behindthebag.net/2018/05/23/
a-colorful-exit-babe-ruths-last-game-film/

DID YOU KNOW?

Babe Ruth's Hall of Fame career began in 1914 with the Red Sox first, before being traded to the rival Yankees. With the Red Sox Babe was considered one of the best left-handed pitchers in baseball. He returned to Boston in 1935 with national league Braves to revive their financial status. The Braves eventually moved to Milwaukee in 1953.

MARCH IN A PARADE

WHAT'S THE DEAL? The city of Boston loves a parade. Whether they are celebrating a sports championship or a historical date like Patriots or Veterans Day, Bostonians come out in full force. Without question, the most popular parade in town is the St. Patrick's Day celebration, a tribute to large Irish population still found in the city today.

DO IT IF: You love a parade or you are Irish for a day.

SKIP IT IF: A few thousand drunk parade goers drinking green beer doesn't sound appealing.

LOCAL ADVICE: Boston's huge St. Patrick's Day Parade, traditionally held each year on the Sunday closest to March 17, attracts up to a million or more spectators, depending on the weather. Spectators stand 12-deep in some areas, especially around the Broadway T station - so arrive early and walk down Broadway to a less-crowded spot if possible.

I DID IT: www.boston-discovery-guide.com/
st-patricks-day-parade.html

DID YOU KNOW?

In addition to Saint Patrick's Day, the parade also celebrates Evacuation Day (an official Boston holiday) in honor of the ousting of British troops from the city on March 17, 1776. As a tribute this historic event, the parade also honors our military services and veterans.

BAKE BEANS

WHAT'S THE DEAL? Bostonians are synonymous with baked beans. Boston is even referred to as Beantown. Turns out, the first colonists learned to cook the beans from the local Native Americans.

DO IT IF: You have dreams of Boston Baked Beans!

SKIP IT IF: You suffer from a Legume Allergy.

LOCAL ADVICE: The Boston style which adds molasses to the recipe is a product of the colonial triangle trade. In colonial New England, baked beans were traditionally cooked on Saturdays and left in the ovens overnight. On Sundays, the beans were still hot, allowing people to indulge in a hot meal and still comply with strict Puritan rules which disallowed cooking on the sabbath. Brown bread and baked beans were a popular meal on Saturdays and Sundays in Massachusetts until at least the 1930s.

I DID IT: ☐ www.food.com/recipe/baked-beans

DID YOU KNOW?

British colonists in New England were the first westerners to adopt the dish from the Native peoples; and were quick to embrace it largely because the dish was reminiscent of peas porridge and because the dish used ingredients native to the New World. They substituted molasses or sugar for the maple syrup, bacon or ham for the bear fat, and simmered their beans for hours in pots over the fire instead of underground.

HIKE THE BLUE HILLS

WHAT'S THE DEAL?   The Blue Hills were so named by early European explorers who, while sailing along the coastline, noticed the bluish hue on the slopes when viewed from a distance. The Natives referred to themselves as Massachusett, or "people of the great hills". There is almost no outdoor sport or activity you cannot do here!

DO IT IF: You want to get back to nature, not far from the city center.

SKIP IT IF: You never leave "Southie."

LOCAL ADVICE: Located only minutes from the bustle of downtown Boston, the Blue Hills Reservation stretches over 7,000 acres from Quincy to Dedham, Milton to Randolph, providing a green oasis in an urban environment. Rising above the horizon, Great Blue Hill reaches a height of 635 feet, the highest of the 22 hills in the Blue Hills chain. From the rocky summit visitors can see over the entire metropolitan area. With its scenic views, varied terrain and 125 miles of trails, the Blue Hills Reservation offers year-round enjoyment for the outdoor enthusiast.

I DID IT: ☐   www.friendsofthebluehills.org

DID YOU KNOW?

In 1893, the Metropolitan Parks Commission purchased the lands of Blue Hills Reservation as one of the first areas set aside for public recreation. Today, the reservation is steeped in both archaeological and historic sites. You will also find the Blue Hills Weather Observatory, a National Historic Landmark, atop Great Blue Hill, with commanding views of the local countryside.

91

TAME A TUNA

WHAT'S THE DEAL? Tuna Fishing out of Boston can only be described as an amazing adrenaline rush. Bluefin Tuna are big, incredibly strong and fight harder than any other fish. The water off the coast is loaded with Bluefin Tuna. It is not uncommon to see hundreds of these ferocious fish crashing the surface busting bait schools throughout the course of a fishing adventure.

DO IT IF: You wish to tame a mighty tuna an perhaps even dine on your catch.

SKIP IT IF: Fishing on the open Sea is not for me.

LOCAL ADVICE: If you have seen and enjoy the TV show Wicked Tuna, this list item might be for you. Bluefin tuna fishing season is historically June through October, so you will be fishing the very same waters as the characters on Television. For the adventure of a lifetime why not try you luck on the ultimate game fish, the Bluefin Tuna. Shaped like a bullet and reaching weights of over a thousand pounds these fish are the premiere game fish in the North Atlantic.

I DID IT: ☐   www.bostonsportfishing.com

DID YOU KNOW?

These 1000 pound Bluefins will test your strength and stamina while providing you with a memory of a lifetime as well as a lot of tuna steaks. The prized meat of a Boston Bluefin is one of the most expensive sushi in the world.

92

FIND THE SCENES FROM THE DEPARTED

WHAT'S THE DEAL? If you are a fan of the movie, you may recognize the neighborhoods where it was filmed.

The picture was loosely based on South Boston mobster Whitey Bulger and an FBI informant. The movie was filmed exclusively in Boston with an all-star cast and won the 2007 Oscar for best picture and director for Martin Scorsese.

DO IT IF: You like mobster movies or movies filmed in Boston or both.

SKIP IT IF: Martin Sheen's Boston accent is offensive to you.

LOCAL ADVICE: If you are a native New Englander of Irish decent, you may have a family member who is Boston P.D. This movie may hit close to home if you have 1 side of the family on one side of the law, with another part of the family who has chosen a more nefarious career. It certainly makes for interesting and sometime contentious family diners, wedding and gatherings.

I DID IT: ☐   www.imdb.com/title/tt0407887

DID YOU KNOW?

Throughout the film, Director Martin Scorsese uses an "X" motif to foreshadow death in a manner similar to Howard Hawks' film Scarface. Examples include shots of cross-beam supports in an airport walkway, the taped windows of a building, and a carpeted hallway floor at the film's end.

93

EXPLORE MT. AUBURN

WHAT'S THE DEAL?   It may be hard to imagine, but the Mt. Auburn Cemetery created a garden and open space movement in the United States. The 170-acre plot of land opened in 1831 and was different from the traditional church burying grounds. It featured open fields, landscaping and dozens of varieties of trees and shrubs, more parklike than a cemetery. Notable burials at Mt. Auburn include poet Henry Wadsworth Longfellow, architect Charles Bulfinch and former Red Sox announcer Curt Gowdy.

DO IT IF: You wish to pay your respects in a parklike setting.

SKIP IT IF: You'll go into a cemetery over your dead body.

LOCAL ADVICE: One of the most amazing aspects of Mount Auburn is the beautiful landscaping and the assortment of flowering trees and flowers. Sometimes when visiting its almost hard to believe you are in a cemetery. If you are in the Boston area in May, this might be the ideal month with the Flowering dogwoods, crabapples, lilacs, and azaleas in full bloom!

I DID IT: ☐   www.mountauburn.org

DID YOU KNOW?

Mount Auburn continues its historic dual role as a sacred site and pleasure ground, serving as both an active cemetery and a "museum" preserving nearly two centuries of changing attitudes about death and commemoration and changing tastes in architecture and landscape design.

94

CRUISE ROUTE 128

WHAT'S THE DEAL? What could be better than putting on the 1970's song "Roadrunner" by Jonathan Richman and the Modern Lovers and cruising the high-tech beltway just west of Boston!

DO IT IF: You like cruising with the radio on like its 1972.

SKIP IT IF: Your car can't go "Faster Miles an hour," you must stop at The Stop and Shop or don't love Massachusetts.

LOCAL ADVICE: Check out the YouTube clip of the song to get an idea what the song is all about if you are not familiar with the tune. There are sold great shots of Boston landmarks as well including the Citgo sign, the Prudential Center, the Boston Long Wharf Marriott Hotel and even the old raised Central Artery Freeway. We mentioned it earlier in the list and been torn down and placed underground by the big dig.

I DID IT: ☐ www.youtube.com/watch?v=Gy88-5pc7c8

DID YOU KNOW?

Johnathan Richman is a Boston area native and has always had a cult following He gained some noteriety when he was featured in the Farrelly Brothers comedy Something about Mary. Richmond and band mate Tommy Larkin comment on the plot while performing their music within the framed action itself. He was the guitar player shot near the end of the hit comedy.

95

TELL EM ROSE SEND YOU

WHAT'S THE DEAL? The Rose Kennedy Greenway, named for the matriarch of the Kennedy clan, was created by the burying of the Central Artery under the streets of Boston from the Big Dig project.

DO IT IF: You live for modern urban greenspaces with lots of fun and free activities.

SKIP IT IF: You suffer from agoraphobia.

LOCAL ADVICE: For one weekend each summer, the Rose Fitzgerald Kennedy Greenway transforms into an eccentric art gallery. It brings together theater, music, sculptures, dance, interactive art and much more into one space. During the FIGMENT Boston weekend, artists across any discipline (meaning no experience required) can install a piece of artwork or put on any performance on the Greenway, if it "somehow engages audience participation." In the past, projects have included mazes, a "Silly Walk Zone," interactive dance routines, motion-detected audio soundscapes, water games and more. Best of all the event is free.

I DID IT: ☐   www.rosekennedygreenway.org

DID YOU KNOW?

The Greenway is named to honor Bostonian Rose Elizabeth Fitzgerald Kennedy,philanthropist, socialite, and a member of the Kennedy family. She was deeply embedded in the Irish Catholic community in Boston, where her father John F. Fitzgerald was mayor. She was the mother of president John F. Kennedy, Senator and Attorney General Robert and Massachusttets Senator Teddy.

LIGHT THE TREE

WHAT'S THE DEAL?   The Boston Christmas Tree is the City of Boston, Massachusetts' official Christmas tree. A tree has been lit each year since 1941, and since 1971 it has been given to the people of Boston by the people of Nova Scotia in thanks for their assistance after the 1917 Halifax Explosion. The tree is lit in the Boston Common throughout the Christmas season.

DO IT IF: You enjoy the Christmas season with a festive tree lighting.

SKIP IT IF: Your nickname is" The Grinch!"

LOCAL ADVICE: There are numerous Christmas Trees that spring up around Boston around the holidays, but the Official Tree on Boston Common has a special significance. In an example of saying thank you for a lending a helping hand, Halifax sends a tree south to say an annual thank you for a good deed from decades earlier. It truly is a sentimental moment to ring in the Christmas season.

I DID IT: ☐   www.boston-discovery-guide.com/ christmas-tree-lighting-ceremonies.html

DID YOU KNOW?

On December 6, 1917 ,the Halifax Explosion severely destroyed much of the city, by the largest man-made explosion up to that time. Boston authorities learned of the disaster by telegraph, and quickly organized and dispatched a relief train by 10 pm to assist survivors.

97

DUMP TEA IN THE HARBOR

WHAT'S THE DEAL? On December 16th, 1773 a band of protestors known as the sons of liberty and disguised as Native Americans, boarded a British vessel in Boston Harbor. The ship was laden with cases from the East India Tea Company and was quickly emptied by the angry mob, tossing the entire cargo into the harbor. Colonists were angered by the recently passed Tea Act because they believed that it violated their rights as Englishmen to "No taxation without representation." Stop by the museum where you too can toss some tea overboard in the very waters the insurrection occurred.

DO IT IF: You want low taxes with maximum representation.

SKIP IT IF: The wastefulness of dumping tea is technically polluting.

LOCAL ADVICE: The Brits loved their tea, so stop by Abigail's café and enjoy a spot. Taste history by sampling some of the 5 teas thrown overboard during the Boston Tea Party, enjoy a glass of refreshing lemonade, iced tea, or a mug of hot or cold apple cider and try tasty treats: assorted scones, cookies, brownies, muffins and pie.

I DID IT: ☐ www.bostonteapartyship.com

DID YOU KNOW?

The Sons of Liberty was a term broadly applied to loosely organized revolutionary bands in the Thirteen American Colonies to advance the rights of the European colonists and to fight taxation by the British government. It played a major role in most colonies in battling the Stamp Act in 1765.

DIP A DONUT

WHAT'S THE DEAL?   The Boston area is famous for a nationally known coffee and donut chain, but this area also has a few local favorite sweet shops. If you are a donut aficionado like me, Kane's in Saugus is hard to beat. It has been in the same location since 1955 and uses locally grown products whenever possible. Some of the local favorites include the Maine Blueberry, the Nut Crunch and the Crème Brule.

DO IT IF: MMM Donuts!!!

SKIP IT IF: You are trying to slim down for bathing suit season.

LOCAL ADVICE: In 1955, Saugus, just north of Boston fell in love for the sweet treats coming out of Kane's Donuts...a mom-and-pop donut shop that opened pre-dawn and served into the early afternoon each day serving locals, first-shifters and most of the local police force, a perfect cup of coffee and a delicious donut with friendly service that brought them back daily. New ownership has breathed life into Kane's with new recipes and 3 locations around greater Boston.

I DID IT: ☐   www.kanesdonuts.com

DID YOU KNOW?

Kane's was   named a top-10 donut destination by The Travel Channel. And since its launch in 2014, Kane's has earned local and national attention for Kane's Gluten Free ...what many consider the best line of gluten-free donuts made by a traditional U.S. donut shop.

CHOW DOWN IN CHINATOWN

WHAT'S THE DEAL? The traditional Chinatown Gate (paifang) with a foo lion on each side is located at the intersection of Beach Street and Surface Road, marking the entrance to one of Boston's most interesting and ever changing neighborhoods.

DO IT IF: You enjoy exploring far east culture, festivals and cuisine.

SKIP IT IF: Live fish in sold on street corners alarms you.

LOCAL ADVICE: A walk through Chinatown is an interesting mixture of sights and sounds. You will see a variety of exotic animals for sale on street corners and market front windows. You will hear Cantonese and Vietnamese being spoken all over the neighborhood and of course there is authentic Chinese food you won't soon forget. One interesting way to learn more about this ever-evolving neighborhood is do a food tour with historical information intertwined with samplings at various dining locations.

I DID IT: ☐ bitesofbostonfoodtours.com/
chinatown-culture-cuisine-tour

DID YOU KNOW?

Part of the Chinatown neighborhood occupies land reclaimed by filling in a tidal basin. The newly created area was settled by a mixed succession of Irish, Jewish, Italian, Lebanese, and Chinese immigrants. Each group replaced the previous one to take advantage of low-cost housing and job opportunities in the area.

100

TOUR THE TOWN BY TROLLEY

WHAT'S THE DEAL? The ubiquitous Old Town Trolleys are easily visible throughout Boston with their distinctive Orange and Green colors. The guides offer great historical tidbits, and the trollies make multiple stops throughout the city, allowing you a great overview of the historical sights, with the option to tour other attractions along the way.

DO IT IF: You want to learn from local guides while being driven to all the local points of interest.

SKIP IT IF: You think you know more than your Boston born and raised tour guide.

LOCAL ADVICE: Our favorite part about doing the old town trolley tours is the flexibility they offer. With multiple stops around the town, hop on and off in multiple historic location than you wish to explore more in depth. Typically trolleys pass every 15 to 20 minutes at each stop to pick up the narration where you left off. Or stay on board if there is a driver/guide that you really enjoy so you get a complete overview and lay of the land, before exploring something that interests you.

I DID IT: ☐ www.trolleytours.com/boston

DID YOU KNOW?

After doing tours in Key West, Florida, the founders of Historic Tours traveled the country to expand their business. Starting with Boston and eventually adding St. Augustine, San Diego, Savannah, Nashville and Washington, DC, Old Town Trolley Tours now boasts over 130 trolleys in 7 cities.

Made in United States
Troutdale, OR
12/11/2023

15651940R00066